THE BOOK OF
Florida Gardening

By PASCO ROBERTS

GREAT*OUTDOORS*
PUBLISHING CO.

4747 TWENTY-EIGHTH STREET NORTH   ST. PETERSBURG, FLORIDA 33714

International Standard Book No. 0-8200-0402-2
Library of Congress Catalog Card No. 62-52630

Manufactured in the United States of America

CONTENTS

Uncle Pasco

UNCLE PASCO of St. Petersburg is a household word in thousands of homes throughout Florida. Above he is shown at the microphone of WSUN, Radio 620, St. Petersburg as he conducts his Garden Club of the Air. Seven years of daily broadcasts served to compile a formidable array of questions and answers, which taxed even the wide experience of Uncle Pasco. The search for knowledge to answer these questions has resulted in an extensive library of Florida gardening information, the best of which is brought to you in this book.

About the Author

Uncle Pasco Roberts began his life devoted to growing things, in North Florida. Actually he farmed as a youth in Bradford County, although he was born in Bristol, Florida in 1898. The name "Pasco" was a gift from Senator Samuel Pasco, who came to Liberty County, Florida, with the Roberts family in 1851. Most of Uncle Pasco's early life was in the Jacksonville area.

From kindergarten days, Uncle Pasco had an eye for things beautiful. As he grew into manhood, his talents branched out into the fields of art, photography, music and horticulture. Sometimes he combined all these talents in one basket, such as using music with his Radio Garden Club and photographing botanical subjects for reproduction in newspapers and magazines.

The radio program entitled *Uncle Pasco's Radio Garden Club* maintained a high rating during the seven-year run over WSUN in St. Petersburg, Fla. and also on WMBR in Jacksonville, Fla. and WFLA in Tampa, Fla. Because of sponsorship variables, Uncle Pasco discontinued in favor of the various writing angles pertaining to plants and gardening.

As garden editor for the years *Sunrise Magazine* circulated, he used a camera with telling effect to illustrate his articles. His book *Sunrise Garden Guide* sold nearly 100,000 copies. Then for many years he made and marketed botanical slides of Florida subjects. Many thousands of these slides are in circulation today, all over the world — and especially in the catalogs of nurseries and seed producers.

This botanical photography experience was the principle factor in cementing contact with thousands of gardening enthusiasts who kept up with the Radio Garden Club activities.

It would be difficult to find a man better grounded — and so well known in his field in Florida, as Uncle Pasco Roberts. His experience in growing things, operating a nursery and then possessing the ability to pass this information along to the public with his camera and typewriter, is unmatched.

In fact there is probably no other man with so many written answers to the questions: "What grows in Florida; how to grow it — and where to get the start." Uncle Pasco has established a lifelong reputation of cheerful assistance to the fledgling gardener. He invites requests — and all inquiries to Great Outdoors will be passed directly to him.

Uncle Pasco lives in St. Petersburg on a beautiful two and a half-acre plot facing a busy street. His wife-mate (known on radio as Aunt Cliff with her Tropical Recipes) is also a photo-finisher and musician. Their estate which includes a marvelous lake, loaded with enormous bass, has more than 2,000 different specimens.

It is from this idyll in the suburbs of St. Petersburg, that Uncle Pasco comes to you through the pages of this book, to help you with your garden — and make Florida beautiful.   R.A.

Foreword

WHAT GROWS in Florida — how to grow it — where to get it — this was the theme of my 2,000 radio broadcasts and the garden pages of the SUNRISE Magazine. My editorial experience plus that of a gardener, nurseryman, and botanical photographer, and the experience of hundreds of plant lovers, horticulturists and plant specialists all over the state and elsewhere — are the very essence of this book.

The many thousands of cards and letters received in the various capacities mentioned, have revealed to me the type of information desired by the largest number of residents. Judging from the mail and by personal contacts all over, I find more interest in the subjects of fast growing trees, shrubs and fruit, also requests for information on lawns and lawn grasses.

The growing of plants in wood-shavings and sawdust was a very popular subject and brought terrific response from all over the globe. The highlights of this method are covered in detail. The sources of supply are mentioned on some items, to help you make contacts or locate items without too much trouble. With the exception of a few plants or garden items, there are of course, many other reliable sources, perhaps right in your own area.

For general use, I have divided Florida into four growing zones. When North Florida is mentioned, it includes areas from the Georgia line southward to Volusia County on the East Coast and Levy County on the West Coast, and all other areas as far west as Pensacola. The lower parts of this zone are also referred to as North Central zone. Central Florida zone starts below Levy County and Seminole or Orange Counties on the East Coast. This is divided however in North Central areas and South Central areas. The southern part includes the following counties: Pasco, Hillsborough, Pinellas, Manatee, Sarasota, Polk, Osceola, Brevard, Indian River, De Soto, Highlands, St. Lucie and parts of Okeechobee. South Florida zone includes everything from the Keys to Fort Myers on the West Coast and Palm Beach on the East Coast. Nearly all of these areas have "pockets" of warm or cold, and you often find "pockets" of varying temperature, and you often find a plant on the "taboo" list growing in such places.

The many interesting plants, flowers, trees, shrubs, vines, orchids, air plants, and other natural beauties of my native state, I have captured in color, and some are reproduced in black and white from my collection of 30,000 Kodachrome slides.

Preparing this book has been a pleasure, and I sincerely hope you will find much useful information among its pages. Happy Gardening!

Sincerely,

Uncle Pasco Roberts.

Your Garden

OUR GARDEN, whether small or large may be a means of relaxation, a hobby, a labor of love or a spiritual uplift. Or it may be even a means of increased revenue. The Hebrew word "adamah" means dust, mould or arable land, hence the name ADAM given to the first man created. The Holy Scriptures reveal that man started in a garden, and will return to the garden, so you see there is a spiritual affinity between man and the soil, and the axiom, "Happy is the man or woman who works with the soil" is an indisputable self-evident truth.

THE SOIL COMES FIRST

No matter what your garden or farm means to you, in order to have success in the growing of plants, you must consider the soil first. You can make a simple test of different areas by taking a handful of soil, wet it and if it packs into a mud pie, it is not very suitable without the addition of soil conditioners. The ideal soil is one that is friable or crumbly, non-packing, slightly moist. The soil experts classify the Southern soils into seven different textures or sizes of soil particles. To help you understand the requirements indicated on seed packets, they are listed as follows:

(1) Very fine sand. (2) Fine sand. (3) Medium sand. (4) Course sand. (5) Fine gravel. (6) Silt. (7) Clay. Other characteristics are as follows:

SAND—Is 85% or more sand.

LOAMY SAND—from 70% to 80% sand.

SANDY LOAM—50% to 70% sand with the remainder silt and clay.

SANDY CLAYLOAM — Between 20% and 35% clay with remainder mostly sand.

CLAY—40% to 60% soil is clay.

SILT—88% or more of the soil is silt.

SILT LOAM—72% to 88% silt and less than 28% clay.

SILTY CLAY LOAM—60 to 72% silt, and less than 40% clay.

SILTY CLAY—40% to 60% silt and less than 60% clay.

LOAM—30% to 50% silt, and 10% to 28% clay, and 50% to 72% sand.

ORGANIC MATTER

Very seldom do you find the ideal soil around the new homes of today, for most of the organic matter (if any) has been plowed or leveled so that none of the top soil is left. Then again much of the soil is "filled-in" with soil taken from sand, shell or dirt pits. The good soil is sold at a premium. Soil near the coast consists mostly of beach sands, or a mixture of everything except soils containing any organic matter.

No matter what the structure of the soil, it can be improved by the addition of humus organic matter, soil conditioners, etc. The word "humus" is a general term applied to the group of substances which form the organic matter of the soil, and which comes from the remains of plants or animals. Peat or the various mosses are examples of organic matter from decayed plants. The various manures are called organic matter, and nearly all types are excellent for the soil, especially those classified as stable or dairy manures. Green manures is a term applied to a group of plants used as "cover crops" and which are plowed under or cut into the soil. The average home garden is too small to utilize many of the plants used in this manner, so composting is suggested.

By composting, you utilize all the waste materials, such as leaves, hulls, peels of many fruits and vegetables, egg shells, seed pods, and nearly all the garbage. In other words almost anything that will decay may be added to a heap. This heap or compost pile may take almost any form or shape, however there are many who insist they must be made this way or that way. Besides the open heap, there can be the enclosed type, such as concrete blocks, bins, etc. Some prefer to dig a hole in the ground two or three feet deep and fill it at random, adding minerals, plant foods, or even commercial fertilizers. One of the simplest ways for a small garden, is to procure one or more tub parts of old washing machines. They can be found around repair departments of appliance stores, or at the city dump. Place the tubs (which have a hole in the center) on three or four bricks, and fill with leaves, hulls, peels, etc., and occasionally pour some soluble plant food on the mixture. In a year or less time you will have usable material to add to the soil.

Most garden supply stores sell ready made composts, all sorts of hulls, etc. so if you prefer you may help supply organic matter almost instantly.

It is a well known fact that "earth worms" help aerate the soil and their presence is a good indication of organic matter. Some add worms to the soil, but if you provide the organic matter first, they will somehow or another find their way to your garden. It is true however, that the addition of what is known as "Activators" will help added matter to decay to become useful as organic matter or humus much more quickly than by the natural method. These bacterial activators are sold under such names as ACTIVO, ACTUMUS, ADCO, COMPOSTO and others.

Besides the vegetable and animal matter, there are a number of other items which will improve the soil. For instance, wood ashes, coal ashes, sawdust, shavings, and of recent years the substance called vermiculite (sold as Terra-Lite or Zonolite) and another called Perlite (sold by building supply houses). Let's consider each in order:

Coal or wood ashes tend to improve the physical properties of the heavier type soils. Hardwood ashes are considered the best, as they also contain a good supply of potash. In beds use about four ounces per square yard.

Sawdust is one of the finest items to provide aeration to the soil and in time become organic matter. It is an ideal mulch for many plants. Old sawdust is best, however new sawdust (pine, cypress or other types) may be used, but you must add more nitrogen, and for this purpose the organic types which are slow acting are recommended. Such include castor pomace, cotton seed meal, tankage, and commercial items like Milorganite or Frazier's compost.

Soluble plant foods are useful, and may be applied once a month during the growing season. With either sawdust or shavings, one of the activators mentioned would be a great help in maturing and causing the quick appearance of earth worms.

What is said of sawdust equally applies to wood shavings. Generally speaking, shavings are easier to procure from your local mills or building supply houses. Most nurseries use them for mulching, but sawdust is preferable to incorporate in the soil, or as a medium to root certain types of plants. (See Propagation)

Vermiculite is an exploded mica and contains no plant food elements and is used strictly for aerating purposes, or as a sterile medium to root plants. Sold as Terra-Lite it is for the soil, as Zonolite is used in plaster and insulation, however either may be used for garden purposes. (See more details on page 10).

Perlite is a very white light-weight material used also in plaster, etc. and excellent for mixing with heavy soils or for rooting of plants. Both vermiculite and perlite have special uses for the gardener and are not expensive.

There is still another soil conditioner which is very useful for sandy or beach soils. It is a product of the phosphate mines and sold as Colloidal (or Pond) Phosphate. It is an excellent material for retaining moisture, or building sandy soils. By using as much as five pounds of Colloidal Phosphate to the planting hole for shrubs like Hibiscus, Jasmines, Pittosporum, and small trees, you not only help hold moisture, but it helps to utilize the plant food elements. Add a good supply of organic matter, compost or fertilizer in with the colloidal phosphate. Sawdust and colloidal phosphate is a good combination for dry sandy areas. Mixed with chicken manure and incorporated in the soil, it is excellent for many plants. It has a tendency to sweeten the flavor of papaya, and many citrus fruits when mixed with organic plant foods. One thing to remember, do not use Colloidal Phospate on top of the ground, as it will cake and resemble dried clay. It is better to mix it with soil so that most of it is two or more inches deep, or mix it with the organic matter and soil used in planting holes. Do not use colloidal phosphate with low wet, mucky or predominantly clay soils. Use gypsum with clay soils.

There are many other soil conditioners that are good for special purposes. Organic gardeners especially like such items as green-sand, marlite, granite rock, rock phosphate, and Hybro-Tite and scores of others sold under special brand names. The majority of these items are reliable, however, it is best to consult your local garden supply houses for information.

So useful is Peat and Spaghnum mosses in soil improvement, and for related purposes, that we will consider them under a separate heading.

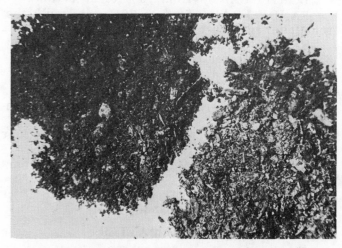

Potting Soil (left) and Commercial Compost (right) using peat, sawdust, leaves, and other organic materials.

Using Sphagnum Moss

ALTHOUGH SPHAGNUM and Peat Moss are classified as two separate things, they are as related as the egg and the chicken, and there is no doubt which one came first. It starts with Sphagnum which is a pale green (sometimes it is almost white) moss which grows and floats in water, and may be found in ponds, or marshes in certain areas of the world. During the process of maturing, the cells increase in size, but do not decay or change in content. Because the interior substance clings to the walls leaving the cells hollow and spongelike, Sphagnum Moss has the ability to soak up and hold large quantities of water.

Agricultural and scientific research reveals that Sphagnum Moss is a very effective and sterile medium for the starting of seeds, bulbs, tubers, etc. without the fear of damping-off, fungi or plant diseases. It was also discovered that it contained penicillin which accounts for its preventative ability.

Sphagnum Moss is excellent for shipping bare-rooted, or potted plants for long distances. Many nurseries and plant growers use it for this purpose, and others use it for the starting of cuttings, or for shipping of rooted cuttings. In recent years the combination of Sphagnum and vinyl plastics (polyethylene) has been used on a large scale for Air-Layering (also called Mossing-off). See chapter on Propagation of Plants.

STARTING SEEDS OR BULBS

Many specialists and agricultural departments make up flats (or other containers) filled with shredded Sphagnum Moss for the starting of seeds, bulbs, tubers, rhizomes, or even cuttings. These containers are generally placed over another container filled with water, and sufficient moisture is absorbed by capillary action, keeping the moss right for the sprouting of seeds, bulbs, etc. In fact it will maintain many plants for a long time, however, it is advisable to transplant when the true leaves appear.

SPHAGNUM AND PEAT

It is not necessary to cover seeds, bulbs or tubers, as they will sprout, take root in the moss, and grow seemingly from air and moisture. Real large bulbs or tubers may be covered with moss an inch or more. The container in this case should be about four inches deep with most of it filled with moss. An ordinary kitchen fork is excellent for lifting seedlings when transplanting.

Coarse ground peat used in commercial compost.

ABOUT CONTAINERS

It is an easy matter to find suitable containers in dime stores, or similar places that sell such things as cake pans. Purchase square or oblong cake pans that are two or three inches deep and punch many holes in the bottom. Break-up a quantity of Sphagnum Moss by hand, or by shredding, and soak it in a nutrient solution made from one of the better soluble plant foods. Line the pans or containers with the dampened moss and you are ready to plant your seeds or bulbs.

Larger containers may easily be made from wire-mesh (half-inch squares) commonly called hardware cloth. With tin-snips you can cut the wire-mesh into square, oblong or even round shapes. The bottom for instance may be two feet square, and the sides, each twenty-four inches long by three inches (or four) deep, can be fastened by the protruding strips or by means of flexible wire. This type of container may be used under a constant fine mist as described in the chapter on Propagation methods, or it may be placed over another container filled with water.

One thing to remember about seeds, bulbs, or seedlings grown by the Sphagnum Moss method, they must not be allowed to dry-out, so this means it is advisable to place all containers in filtered sunlight or light shade. If the Constant Mist method is used, the containers may be placed in full sun.

Using Sphagnum Moss

PEAT MOSS AND ITS USES

Peat the final product from the break-down of Spagnum Moss (and sometimes other vegetation) is found in many areas of the world in large quantities.

SPHAGNUM AND PEAT

As a general rule the better grades come from colder climates, however some very fine Peat is found in Florida and Georgia and the Gulf States. Some of the very best grades sold in the dry form come from Germany and Canada. This is usually processed and is said to be free of weeds, seeds and other obnoxious materials, and termed "horticultural grade" peat. You may buy it in bags or bales from nurseries or garden supply stores.

One thing to keep in mind about the dry or horticultural grades of peat, is that it doesn't contain the friendly bacteria or micro-organisms so effective and much needed in most soils. You can help hasten the bacterial action by adding such things as worm castings, and activators sold under such brand names as Activo, Actumus, Composto and many others. Mixing with the various manures such as poultry, cow or stable manures is another good way to hasten bacterial action. Many people add the dry peat to composts, which in time becomes effective in whatever capacity it is used.

In some areas, it is possible to buy wet peat from local or nearby peat pits, or from nurseries or garden stores. Some may be very good and contain live micro-organisms etc., but again some may contain unwanted weed seeds and other harmful materials.

PEAT IN POTTING SOILS

Potting soils are made by many nurseries for their own use, or for the public. In fact there are many firms who specialize in the making of potting soils for all kinds of plants. In the garden departments of many stores you will find almost any type you need for the general run of plants. The base of most of the formulas sold is peat. It is generally composted in huge piles, and put through shredders or grinders and bagged for public use.

SPHAGNUM AND PEAT

Nurserymen and many plant specialists make seed or cutting beds with a mixture of sharp (diamond-cut) sand or coarse washed sand and peat, using the half and half formula. Some prefer a mixture of sand, peat and vermiculite using equal parts of each. There is a very fine grade of coarse sand known as Lake Wales sand available in many areas of Florida and South Georgia.

PEAT AS A MULCH

Peat has been used for many years as a mulch for azaleas, camellias, gardenias, rhododendrons, and many other of the extreme acid-loving plants. Horticultural grades have a tendency to dry out quickly, so it is safer to use a composted material that contains organic matter in abundance. Leaf mold, oak leaves, Java Plum leaves, seed pods of the Mothers Tongue (*Albizzia lebbek*) tree are all highly recommended to cover a layer of peat when used as a mulch. Well matured sawdust and peat mixed together is also an excellent mulch material. To this add Milorganite, sludge or castor pomace for additional nitrogen needed.

MIRACLE ROOTING MEDIUMS
Vermiculite

Vermiculite, a non-metallic mineral, was once considered worthless in the ore form. Thomas H. Webb who discovered this mineral in 1824 found that when it was subjected to 2,000° Fah. the microscopic water particles trapped between the laminations would turn to steam and cause a curious expanding motion similar to the vermicular action of worms. Hence the name Vermiculite. Today it is offered to the public under the brand name of TERRA-LITE for horticultural use, and ZONO-LITE as a plaster aggregate and usually is found in building supply houses. The horticultural grade sold by garden supply houses is best for plants, however Zono-Lite may be used safely, the main difference being that it contains a good percentage of powdery vermiculite rather than the more uniform granules of Terra-Lite.

The granules of Terra-Lite remind you of cork to the "feel", but they can be rubbed into powder when dry, or into a greasy substance when wet. When used in seed flats or beds, it is best not to firm or tamp it when it is wet, otherwise you might ruin the material. Terra-Lite is extremely light in weight, a two-bushel bag only weighs approximately 15 lbs. It is a sterile medium for nearly all plant uses, whether for starting seeds, bulbs, cuttings, air-layering or as a mulch. When used dry, it is excellent for storing bulbs, roots and tubers.

The rooting of cuttings in vermiculite is a simple matter. Just fill almost any type container (which can provide some drainage) to a depth of from two to six inches, and pour enough water

Miracle Rooting Mediums

or nutrient solution to make it damp, but not soggy. Place cuttings of three to six inches in length so that one third to one half is in the vermiculite. Large hardwood cuttings of such plants as the Hibiscus, Bougainvillas, Crotons, Oleanders and a host of others do well in plain vermiculite, or half and half of sand and vermiculite.

If your cuttings are rather large and top-heavy, do not use vermiculite alone, but mix with sand and peat, so that it is able to support them upright.

You may lift cuttings almost anytime to note their progress. It is an easy matter to re-set them in flat or container.

Seeds germinate faster Virtually no damping off

Fig. 1

Great mass of hair roots in half the time.

Fig. 2

Perfect as a mulch for all plants.

Fig. 3

Stored bulbs stay firm and plump.

Fig. 4

PERLITE

Another very useful substance for the starting of cuttings, seeds, and to some degree in potting mixtures is sold by building supply houses under the general name of PERLITE (also sold under trade names.) Scientific references state that Perlite (or Pearlstone) is an unusual form of siliceous lava composed of small spherules about the size of bird shot or small peas. It has a grayish white or soft pearly luster color. Like vermiculite it is extremely light in weight, and not expensive. For horticultural purposes, it may be used in the same manner and for the same general purpose as vermiculite, however, it provides better support to many cuttings, and many plant specialists prefer it for the Constant Mist system of Propagation described in this book. Mixed with a good potting soil or top soil it helps provide better aeration, therefore is excellent for transplanting. Perlite does not break down after use, so it has this advantage over vermiculite. It should be sterilized however, if used more than once. Perlome sold in certain areas is a similar material and equally effective.

VERMICULITE — Light weight sterile medium, with many horticultural uses.

PERLITE — Light weight (plaster aggregate) useful in propagation of plants.

Propagation of Plants

There are many methods and variations used for the propagation of plants. The largest majority are started from cuttings or slips that are inserted in soil or some of the rooting mediums mentioned. Although many gardeners, or plant growers, have their own pet system or method, we will describe some of the most successful or logical ones for general use. First of all let us consider the selection of wood to be used for the cutting beds, etc. Green leafy tip cuttings that are not woody, are generally called SOFTWOOD (or Greenwood). They are also referred to as SLIPS. The Spring flush growth usually makes excellent cutting material. This type of cutting should seldom be more than 3 to 5 inches long, and contain two eyes at least. After cutting to length, trim off the lower leaves. Be sure and make basal cuts through the eye or node or half an inch below the node. Slanted cuts are used for most plants, however for soft plants like geraniums, daturas, and the various succulents, it is best to make straight across cuts.

HALF-RIPE cuttings implies that the wood is neither soft or hard, but more or less in between. An easy way to test whether soft or half-ripe is by bending the cutting, and should it snap instead of giving, it is considered SOFTWOOD.

HARDWOOD cuttings are obtained from old growth of plants or trees. This type usually comes from deciduous plants, which means those that lose their leaves in the Fall or Winter months. In Florida not all trees or shrubs are deciduous, however a good many do lose their leaves for a period. Hardwood cuttings are usually taken in the Autumn before cold or freezing weather. They should be from 6 to 12 inches long. Shorter cuttings have a tendency to dry out quickly.

Some plants require callousing of their cuttings before placing in containers, beds or nursery rows. The procedure is to tie from 25 to 100 cuttings in a bundle, and place in a prepared sand pit about two feet deep, leaving the top ends about 4 inches above the soil level. The bottom of the hole is filled with dry sand (coarse sand is best) deep enough to allow your cuttings to extend above soil as suggested. It takes from 3 to 8 weeks to properly callous the general run of hardwood cuttings. You may examine them from time to time to determine if ready to set in beds, or rows, etc. It is possible to start some of your favorite plants from hardwood cuttings placed directly in the soil. In warm areas like Florida the list is quite extensive, and includes the following: Althea, (Rose of Sharon), Abelia, Catalpa, Climbing Roses, Deutzias, Forsythias, Grapes, Privet, Ligustrums (small leaf types), and Spirea.

CUTTINGS IN WATER

Many plants will root in just plain water, or water with a little nutrient added. House plants like Philodendrons, Chinese Evergreen, English Ivy, Nephthytis, Pothos, Coleus, and Hoya (Wax Plant vine) root easily, however they root more easily in builder's sand, and other mediums such as vermiculite and perlite. Such plants as the Acalyphas (including Copper Leaf), Morning Glory Bush (*Ipomoea leptophylla*), Oleander, may also be started in water. Rainwater is preferred by plants mentioned.

ROOTING LEAF CUTTINGS

If you have a rare plant, or very little cutting material, you may start many plants from what is termed leaf cuttings. These include the stem with an auxiliary bud at the base. From such plants as the Hibiscus, Azalea, Ixora, Bougainvillea, Chrysanthemum, etc., you may obtain cutting material up to 20 inches in length, that may be cut into proper lengths, and then have enough leaf cuttings to start even more plants. Just select a single leaf which has a leaf-bud at the base, and cut it from the plant (in manner of shield budding) and place in rooting medium selected. For quicker and better roots treat the lower end of the cutting with a hormone powder like Naph, Rootone, or Hormonex. Leaf-bud cuttings from the following plants usually respond to this treatment: Gesneriads like the African Violet, Gloxinia, Episcias, Streptocarpus, Achimines and others. Also the various Bryophyllums or Kalanchoes, Sedums, Crassulas, Crotons, Euphorbias, Peperomias, Acalyphas, Camellias, Clerodendrons, Forsythias, Sanchezia, Viburnum, Geraniums, Oleanders, Apples, and Blackberries. The Hoya (5 or 6 kinds) which is sometimes called the Wax Flower Vine is generally started from leaf cuttings using one or two healthy leaves with a portion of stem (part of vine) left to insert in cutting bed. This is an excellent climbing vine for indoors in cooler climates, or outdoors for either trellis, containers, or to climb or circle such palms as the Date or Phoenix types.

CONSTANT MIST METHOD

The Constant Mist system is perhaps the most widely used for the commercial propagation of plants. Special spray heads allow a very fine mist to cover cuttings in containers or prepared beds. It is referred to as constant, because it is allowed to run all day long (or even 24 hours a day), although after a certain length of time, depending on the progress of the root formation, the spraying or misting period may be reduced to 4 to 8 hours each day. Each spray head covers ap-

Propagation of Plants

proximately 4 square feet, and it is centered over the cutting bed. One head is sufficient for the average gardener, and to save a lot of pipe and head installation, it is possible to purchase models that stick into the ground at any angle, and you simply attach your garden hose to the coupling provided. Garden supply stores in some areas supply one known as the MAGIC MIST. If your requirements call for more than one head, then it is a good idea to visit your garden supply store or a large nursery, and study the installations. Usually the spray heads require half-inch pipe which may be bought in four or six foot lengths. The average cutting bed is about 4 feet wide, and of course the length depends on how many heads are to be used. Although the spray heads are allowed to run all day or constantly, very little is added to your water bill.

PREPARING BEDS

Plant growers usually make beds on top of the ground and fill them with one or more of the rooting mediums described in these pages. These beds can be made easily by using concrete blocks laid side by side the entire length, and then across the ends to form an enclosure. Some line the bottom with pieces of tin or metal to prevent any long roots from going into the soil, and to make lifting of rooted cuttings easier. The enclosure is filled with either the following: Sawdust to the depth of six inches . . . or it may be all gravel such as sold for poultry use and sometimes termed Turkey gravel . . . or it may be four inches of builder's (coarse) sand and two inches or more Perlite or Vermiculite . . . or one third sand, one third peat (shredded) and one third Perlite or Vermiculite. Still another mixture that works well is half sawdust and half coarse white sand. There are many other variations in use, but all mixtures mentioned are dependable.

Some plant growers use prepared flats or containers instead of beds. You can use buckets, pans, wooden boxes, wash-tubs, and many other items filled with any of the rooting mediums or mixtures mentioned and get results. The containers are placed in a circle under the mist. The depth, of course, depends on the length of cuttings used. One thing to remember, no matter which method or variation is used, you get better results with Mist Propagation if your containers or beds are in full sun. You may inspect the progress of rooting at any time.

NOTE: Not all garden stores sell Mist Propagation Spray heads, so you may have to make inquiries from nurserymen or wholesale supply houses.

GROUND LAYERING

There are two methods of layering plants in general use. Ground layering applies to plants and vines whose lower limbs or branches either touch the ground or can be pegged down in some manner to obtain roots. Many plants have limbs or branches that hug the ground and take root naturally, while others may need the assistance of man. It is a simple matter in most cases, to bend a lower branch down to the earth and peg it down with small wooden or metal stakes and cover with soil. Sometimes it is better to make a slanted cut or slit on the underside of branch before pegging and covering. When roots are much in evidence, you may sever from the parent plant and let grow for a month or 6 weeks, or lift the rooted portion with some soil intact and transplant in a container. Sometimes it is not possible to lift with soil intact, however it may be transplanted and put under the constant mist (or in the shade) for a few weeks.

Numerous plants form roots by mere contact with soil and all along the entire length of the limb or vine will be found root formations that can be utilized for cuttings. The beautiful flowering shrub (with orchid color blossoms) called the *Honckenya ficifolia* is an ideal shrub of this type. Many of the Alternantheras, Jasmines, Angels Trumpet (Datura), Morning Glory Bushes (*Ipomoea leptophylla*) and certain roses produce rooted lower limbs or branches. You will discover many plants of "self-rooting types" as you walk around gardens, estates, parks, etc. Make a note for future use.

Ground-layering up in the air is a variation that is useful at times. Just elevate a box or container filled with soil or rooting medium high enough to make contact with a selected limb or vine. Make cuts on the underside and peg it down as mentioned for soil method.

AIR LAYERING OF PLANTS

For centuries the Chinese propagated plants on living trees, shrubs and vines by just removing a certain amount of the bark and outer layers of a selected limb and covering with a dampened moss covered with bamboo or other things to hold the moisture. This system with variation came into use in this country under the name of "MOSSING-OFF" and is still called that by many old timers.

The late Col. Wm. R. Grove of Laurel, Fla. began experiments using polyethylene plastic as the outside covering and sphagnum moss for inside and developed what is now known as the "AIRWRAP Method" of air-layering of plants. This method is now in general use by plant growers all over the world and is particularly useful to obtain large plants in a matter of a few weeks.

Propagation of Plants

AIR WRAP METHOD IN DETAIL

STEP 1. Select a limb from one-half inch to three inches (or even more on certain plants) in diameter, and one with a symmetrical top, leaf and branch formation. With a sharp knife remove the bark and cambium layer (this is the thin layer of greenish tissue between the bark and wood) from the limb selected. The length of cut is usually about an inch or more, or at least one-and-a-half times the diameter of limb. Spread a quantity of commercial hormone powder such as Naph, Rootone, etc., over the entire cut portion. Some prefer to soak the moss in a hormone or nutrient solution. It works either way.

STEP 2. Soak a quantity of sphagnum moss in water or nutrient solution. Wring out enough moss to form a ball to cover the treated cut portion. The moss should be moist, but not dripping. About two inches in diameter is enough for small limbs and cuts.

STEP 3. Cut the patented AIRWRAP Plastic into pieces measuring 7x8 inches for average run of plants. Polyethylene plastic may also be used to cover moss. Holding the ball of moss with one hand, bring the plastic piece over so that the edges meet and there is enough to lap slightly. Twist the end of plastic as tight as possible and tie with pure rubber band or grafting strips. Airwrap or white polyethylene plastic is semi-transparent making it possible to observe the root formation from time to time. It is also flexible enough to allow the passage of respiratory gases. If the moss and plastic are put on properly, there is no need for any additional watering.

NOTE: Most garden supply stores can furnish the AIRWRAP Kit of all necessary materials, or the plastic and moss separately.

STEP 4. After applying moss and plastic, tieing, etc., all you have to do is to wait from two to six weeks for most plants, however there are some that may take longer. You can observe the white roots that form in the moss, as they are visible enough thru the transparent plastic to indicate when there are sufficient to be removed from parent plant. More roots are generally formed on the side that received the most shade. If no roots are visible within four weeks, it may be because of the failure to follow instructions, or the wrong season of the year for air-layering. One good rule to follow for successful rooting, is to apply the air-layering method when the sap is flowing. There are however a number of plants that respond at almost any season of the year. About 60 to 75% of plants and shrubs will respond to air-layering methods. Those that are classified as succulent, or plants with a milky-sap, are not recommended for this manner of propagation.

REMOVING THE ROOTED BRANCHES

When you have determined that the root formation is sufficient, your final step is to remove the plastic and sever the rooted portion with moss intact. First make a cut below the ball of moss leaving an inch to inch-and-a-half stub at lower end. Remove the plastic covering, but be careful not to disturb roots or moss. To compensate for shock it is best to trim off half of the leaves from the top of the newly rooted plant, which may be transferred to a container filled with good top soil or potting soil mixtures. Just remember, the roots and all the ball of moss must be intact when transplanting, and be careful when filling the soil in container not to break off roots. (See Fig. 5)

Fig. 1   Fig. 2   Fig. 3   Fig. 4   Fig. 5

Florida Lawns

NO MATTER whether you have a modest or palatial home, estate or building, it usually takes a beautiful lawn to give it the proper setting. The lawn is the first consideration to most people, after building or purchasing a home or rental property. The selection of lawn grasses is sometimes a problem to the newcomer to Florida, or even to those who have resided here a long time. One thing is certain—there is no perfect lawn grass for every location, however with a little observation of existing lawns, and advice from lawn experts, you should be able to establish a beautiful lawn in any area of the state.

First of all—let's consider the various kinds of lawn grasses suitable for the various soils of our state, and where and why they should be planted. Lawn experts claim there are six species of grass that are used for Florida lawns. Four species have been used so long that they are considered "old standards". In alphabetical order they are BERMUDA, CARPETGRASS. CENTIPEDEGRASS, and ST. AUGUSTINEGRASS. The two remaining species are the newly exploited BAHIA grasses and the various ZOYSIA grasses.

BERMUDAGRASS (*Cynodon dactylon*) is perhaps the most common of all lawn grasses in this area. It is a deep-rooted grass that usually comes up where it is not wanted, and is rather hard to control. It will stand heavy traffic and is very useful along the seacoasts. The common Bermudas will not tolerate much shade, therefore it should be considered strictly a grass for full sun locations. If you insist on a Bermuda lawn, it can be established within four months from sprigs, runners or, in other words, from vegetative plantings. Many firms sell Bermuda seed, and there is quite a variance even in the common Bermudas. All the Bermudas, whether common or hybrids, require more plant food applications than other types of lawn grasses. The older or most common types also require more frequent mowings.

IMPROVED BERMUDAS

In recent years there has been considerable improvement in the BERMUDA grasses. In fact, they now have so many virtues that they offer a lot of competition with the other popular lawn grasses. One of the most popular ones in Florida is called the ORMOND BERMUDAGRASS. With an adequate nitrogen fertilization it makes an ideal blue-green lawn. With a low nitrogen fertilization, it is susceptible to a fungus known as "dollarspot". Many firms now offer sprigs or sod of the ORMOND BERMUDAGRASS. With proper feeding and frequent watering a truly beautiful lawn can be established within six to 10 weeks. The ORMOND and nearly all the other newer hybrids will produce a permanent turf much quicker than other grasses. All are strickly "sun" grasses, and should not be planted in shade.

ORMOND BERMUDA — Fast growing, fine texture.

ORMOND BERMUDAGRASS is a fine texture grass, so if you prefer medium or fine texture then consider the EVERGLADES No. 1 or the TIFLAWN (Tifton 57) which are vigorous growing grasses of dark-green color. Everglades No. 1 has a medium fine texture, while the Tiflawn is still finer and more upright in growth, and also more resistant to leaf-spot disease than Ormond. There is another popular hybrid with a paler green color known as the BAYSHORE BERMUDAGRASS.

Much credit goes to the Coastal Plain Experiment Station of Tifton, Georgia for the many fine Bermuda hybrids that have originated there and some of which have proven worthy for Florida conditions. One of their newest releases now available in some parts of the state is a fine texture grass with beautiful green color known as TIFWAY (or Tifton No. 419). Dr. Roy Blair, a well known grass specialist of Florida, is responsible for a number of new hybrids. His VELVET BERMUDAGRASS has a fine texture comparable to the finer Zoysia grasses.

All in all the once "muchly cussed" Bermudas have been so improved that they are much in demand for that sunny location.

CARPETGRASS (*Axonopus affinis or compessus*) is a fast growing grass from seed and suitable for damp soils (semi-wet places). Seed may be purchased from garden supply houses or seed stores, however the largest majority of areas of Carpetgrass started voluntarily. They produce tall seed spikes that are scattered easily, and many seeds are blown into moist soil. As a lawn grass it requires frequent mowings. It is a coarse texture grass with a good green color, and at a short distance it is often mistaken for St. Augustinegrass.

Florida Lawns

CENTIPEDEGRASS (*Eremochloa ophiuroides*) is one of the most widely used lawn grasses in North and Central Florida, also most of the Gulf Coast states. It is considered a "low-level" maintenance grass, for it seems to thrive in fairly dry soils without much attention and requires but little plant food. On top of all this, it requires less mowing than almost any other lawn grass. Once established it will crowd out most weeds and such grasses as Bermuda and St. Augustine. It is not recommended for use in shade, however light shade of open branched trees does not interfere with its growth. Do not plant in real sandy areas or along the seacoast where there is a salt spray. The green-stemmed variety is best for all-around use. Yellow and red stemmed varieties are sometimes encountered. Sometimes the better strain seeds are offered by dealers, however sprigs and sod are available in suitable areas. One application of a complete fertilizer in October is about all the requirements needed for Centipedegrass. Soluble type plant foods can be used two or three times a year if you need a booster. A good soaking

CENTIPEDE — Medium texture grass, suitable for sunny locations.

with water will usually revive any dead-looking Centipede lawns.

Centipede takes on a brownish color during the colder months. Some lawn specialists recommend sowing with Italian Rye Grass during this period to maintain a good green colored lawn.

Sod webworms and Fall armyworms and fungi are the major pests of Centipedegrasses. Although it is seldom bothered by these pests, it is not immune by any means. Rainy or muggy weather may cause trouble now and then. Applications of neutral copper, Dithane, or Scott's SCUTL will control fungi. Use KWIT for control of ants, worms, fire-ants, mole crickets, leaf hoppers and even Summer Chinch Bug.

FLORATINE ST. AUGUSTINEGRASS — New low-growing grass suitable for sun or shade.

Years ago a grass known as St. Augustinegrass was introduced to Florida from St. Augustine, Texas. In less than 50 years it became the number one grass for most of the state. ST. AUGUSTINEGRASS (*Stenotaphrum secundatum*) is a rather coarse grass that produces a succulent type of leaf growth and running stems on the surface of the ground. Flower-stems up to 8 inches long are sometimes produced if left un-mowed, but seldom any seed is formed. Therefore propagation is either from cuttings, runners or sod. The reason that this grass became so popular is its versatility. It can be used in sun or shade, is tolerant to considerable salt spray, withstands light frosts, grows on poor or rich soil and with proper maintenance it will stay green longer than most other grasses.

More than 25 different strains of St. Augustinegrass have been reported by lawn experts, and some claim they are more immune than others to such pests as the Chinch Bug, the No. 1 enemy. One of the strains was BITTER BLUE and the largest percentage of sod that has been planted in the last 30 years is perhaps of this strain. Bitter Blue St. Augustinegrass has about 10 to 15 nodes per foot in comparison with 5 to 10 nodes found on the common variety. Leaves are shorter and darker green color than the common type. This results in a denser turf. There is a type used for pasture grass known as ROSELAWN St. Augustine, and very often it is sold for lawn grass. It produces tall rank vegetation suitable for pasturages, but not for quality lawns.

A new St. Augustine grass from the Florida Agricultural Experimental testing grounds has been released and named FLORATINE ST. AUGUSTINEGRASS. Data indicates it is a low-growing fine textured variety with a real blue-green color. It has more tolerance to close mowing than the others. Tolerance is ½ inch. For more

Florida Lawns

information on this newest variety write to University of Florida Agricultural Experiment Station at Gainesville, Fla., and ask for circular S-123 called FLORATINE ST. AUGUSTINEGRASS by Nutter and Allen, or contact your County Agent.

Liberal applications of high-nitrogen fertilizers are necessary for all the strains of St. Augustine grasses, especially if the soil is on the sandy side. Scott recommends an extra heavy feeding in October and a normal feeding in December. Spreaders with dial settings on them (such as Scotts Spreader) are useful in getting the right amount or proportions on your lawn.

In the past 10 years the invasion by chinch bugs in almost all areas of Florida has caused the popularity of St. Augustinegrass to go down, down and down. Of course this hysteria could have been prevented if first of all you had provided plenty of organic materials in your soil, and proper feeding to make vigorous growth. Now comes this new FLORATINE variety and perhaps we will see another boom in St. Augustinegrass.

* * * *

BAHIAGRASSES (*Paspalum notatum*) have become some of the most popular of newer grasses in recent years. There are many kinds of Bahias on the market, and some such as the common Bahia are used for pasture grass. We will consider three others suitable for lawns namely: ARGENTINE, PENSACOLA and PARAGUAYAN. All three develop deep root systems in sandy soils, making them suitable for dry conditions. They also form a coarse open turf that looks better from a distance. During the summer, tall heavy seed spikes are produced.

PENSACOLA BAHIGRASS — Easily started from seed.

ARGENTINE BAHIAGRASS does well in southern parts of Florida. A very coarse grass however. PENSACOLA Bahia has the finest texture of all three and does well all over the state. The PARAGUAYAN Bahia texture is intermediate between Argentine and Pensacola varieties. The last two are best for lawns in general. Pensacola maintains the best green color during the winter months, but Paraguayan forms the most dense turf. All the Bahias are established from seed. Because of the coarseness, it is often hard to mow Bahia lawns with reel-type mowers.

* * *

ZOYSIAGRASSES are sometimes called the miracle grasses, and right now they are enjoying the top spot in popularity in Florida and most of Eastern seaboard states as far north as Washington, D.C. and all along the Gulf area. ZOYSIA (*Zoysia spp.*) is relatively slow-growing in comparison to the other grasses we have mentioned, however they do form a dense fine-textured turf of extraordinary beauty. Because of their shallow root system, they seem to do their best in heavier soils, or soils that have been amended with organic matter, clay or vermiculite. Before describing the various Zoysias being advertised, they are not immune to insects or disease, as some of the ads would have you believe. In fact the fungus attacks some 40 years ago prevented them from gaining any recognition in Florida. This however does not apply to some of the newer varieties, for judging from the lawns I have seen the past 5 or 6 years, they are the acme of beauty.

The most commonly planted Zoysia is known as MANILAGRASS or *Zoysia Matrella*. It is very slow-growing and often requires two or more seasons to establish a dense turf. Selected strains are known as FLAWN or RUGLAWN.

JAPANESE LAWN GRASS or *Zoysia japonica* is the only one that can be started from seed, and the seeds are rather scarce and expensive. It is a low-growing perennial that spreads by aboveground runners and shallow root-stocks. Once established it forms a dense turf that resists weed invasion and is seldom bothered with insects or disease. It does well as far north as Philadelphia and westward to San Francisco, Calif. Most Zoysia japonica lawns are started from sprig planting of the stems, or by spot sodding. Sometimes it takes 3 to 4 growing seasons to establish. MEYER ZOYSIAGRASS (or Z-52) was one of the first of the improved Zoysias made available to the turf industry. It's texture is coarser than Zoysia matrella (but finer than Centipedegrass). It has good resistance to the brown patch fungus, turns brown and becomes dormant with the first frost, but still is not the best for Florida conditions.

Florida Lawns

EMERALD ZOYSIA (Fine Textured)

EMERALD ZOYSIAGRASS as the name indicates is a deep green color, and one of the best fine-textured types for Florida. Compared to the others it has a more vigorous horizontal growth, and under ideal growing conditions will make a lawn in one season, provided that the sprigs are placed end to end in rows 4 inches apart. It is a hybrid between the Japanese lawngrass and Mascarene grass (*Zoysia tenuifolia*).

Give Zoysia grasses a heavy feeding in October and a normal one in December.

OTHER USEFUL GRASSES

There are many other suitable grasses for certain types of lawns, and some that supplement the regular species described. For instance, ITALIAN RYEGRASS(*Lolium multiflorum and perenne*) is not exactly a true lawn grass, but is used during the Winter months to keep established lawns (of grasses described) looking like a true green lawn. Ryegrass mixtures sold in this area are usually a mixture of annual, intermediate and perennial types of rye grass. Besides being used with established lawns, it is useful while getting regular grasses established. On sloping areas, you can use a small amount of ryegrass to help prevent soil erosion. Many use ryegrass to cover bald spots temporarily. Instructions for sowing ryegrass may be found in the Garden Calendar section for October.

* * * *

DICHONDRA (*Dichondra repens and Carolinensis*) is used as a lawn in Southern California, and some may be found in Florida. This is not a grass but a perennial that forms a low, dense mat under certain conditions. It doesn't require much fertility, but likes a lot of moisture. The leaves of DICHONDRA are kidney-shaped and are pale to deep green in color. It thrives in sun or shade. In the shade it takes on a darker color, seldom grows over an inch to inch-and-half high, but is sometimes stemmy and will crowd out other vegetation. Good to crowd out bermudagrass. Two types of Dichondra are found in this country, one a native to Carolina and surrounding areas, another a native to California and Western areas. Seeds from both types are offered to the public in packets or in bulk. Dichondra often comes up voluntarily in many lawns, and is often mistaken for the dollar-plant (which has shiny and thick leaves). Like all things, it has its uses.

* * *

A very useful plant for borders along the street where no grass will grow, or to use to fill bare spaces is one often sold as MONDO GRASS. This is misleading, for it is not a lawn grass and its right name is OPHIOPOGON (*Ophiopogon japonica*) or Lilyturf. It might be classed as a ground-cover, and as such it is very effective. Grows to 10 or 12 inches high and bears purple to white flowers on upright spikes. Will grow in shade or sun and in poor or rich soils. Propagated by division and sometimes by seeds.

HOW TO MAKE A BETTER LAWN

Before breaking up your soil, there are a few important things to do first. If the home has just been built or if there is no existing lawn, then it is a good idea to have the top 4 to 6 inches of soil pushed aside until the sub-soil grading operations are completed. Do not bury any debris such as bricks, stones, cement, boards, paper, etc. Install drains if sub-soil is poorly drained. You can usually check with the neighbors about standing water during the rainy seasons.

If you plan to have large shrubs or trees in the lawn, it is a good idea to install a few short tiles upright (and fill with gravel) so that you may feed the root systems in years to come.

Now with the top soil that was pushed aside incorporate plenty of organic matter such as compost, peat, manures, sewage sludge, decomposed sawdust, or such additives as peanut hulls, cocoa shells, buckwheat shells. If your soil is on the sandy side, or it is mostly filled-in land then add 100 lbs. of Colloidal Phosphate to each 1,000 square feet area. This is a fine clay-like substance (from Phosphate mines) that helps hold moisture and makes added plant foods more effective. Do not use with clay or damp soils. Remember the better the foundation the less trouble you will have later. If you don't want to take the trouble or cost of providing a good organic foundation, then it is best to plant low-fertility lawn grasses such as Centipede, Bermuda of the common type, or Bahia. If it is not convenient to have the top soil pushed aside and later mixed with organic materials, then the next best procedure is to work the top four inches of soil with a spade, plow,

Florida Lawns

disk or with a machine such as the Roto-Hoe. Do not work soil when it is full of moisture. You may want your soil tested to see whether it is acid or alkaline. This helps determine if lime or other amendments are needed. You can buy simple soil testing kits from your garden store. Most soils need applications of lime, and the amount to apply will vary with the original acidity of the soil and the type of soil. Dolomite or dolomitic ground limestone which contains magnesium and calcium is best. I might add that Colloidal Phosphate mentioned also helps in this respect. Some of the lime can be added with the topsoil mixture, and usually a little is put on top of prepared soil, but before the final finish grade is established.

* * *

After the soil has been raked and prepared for planting, it is a good idea to let it stand for 10 or 12 days to allow the newly exposed weeds to germinate. You can apply a good weed killer and then sow seed or set sprigs, runners or sod. Better read instructions furnished by the various brands of weed killers available.

* * *

If you start your lawn from seed, be sure it is not a windy day. It is better to use a lawn spreader for this purpose. Most stores will rent you a spreader if you don't intend to buy one. When you have finished sowing, rake the seed into the soil to a depth of about 1/8 of an inch. Some roll the beds after a good raking. For best results use a fairly lightweight roller. (They can be rented also).

It takes from 2 to 3 lbs. of seed for Bahia or Bermuda grasses for each 1,000 square feet. Carpetgrass takes 3 to 4 lbs. for same area. The best time to sow seed is in the Spring.

* * *

For vegetative planting it will take 10 square feet of nursery sod or one bushel of stolons for Bermuda lawns per each 1,000 square feet. Plant in Spring or Summer. For Carpetgrass it takes 8 to 10 square feet of sod. Same for Centipedegrass. Plant either in Spring or Summer. For the Zoysia grasses it takes 30 square feet of sod when plugging, or 6 square feet of sod when sprigging.

* * *

FERTILIZERS AND APPLICATIONS

Bermudagrass, Zoysias and St. Augustinegrass make their maximum growth in hot weather, or in other words during the Summer. These warm season grasses are variable as to the amount of nitrogen requirements, more so than the cool season types. It takes from 5 to 10 lbs. of actual nitrogen per 1,000 sq. ft. per year for Bermudagrasses. This is applied in 3 to 5 applications from early Spring until Fall. St. Augustine and Zoysias require less nitrogen than Bermuda, but more than Carpet, Centipede or Bahiagrasses.

Nitrogen is required to produce good green color in lawn grasses and other plants. Most lawn formulas contain both organic and inorganic types of nitrogen. Organic nitrogen costs more per unit of actual nitrogen than inorganic nitrogen, but it releases its nutrient value to the grass more slowly and gives more uniform stimulation over longer periods. Organic nitrogen is available in processed sludge, Milorganite, tankage, cottonseed meal, soybean meal, and many waste byproducts. Inorganic nitrogen or fertilizers are available as dry materials (such as standard farm fertilizers) or as liquid or dry concentrates that must be diluted with water before they are applied.

In purchasing fertilizers for lawns, it is best to buy what is known as LAWN SPECIALS. Of course the better ones cost more, but they also contain more organic sources of nitrogen and plant foods. Most well known brands are reliable and each usually contains instructions for applying. Many soluble plant foods are useful for lawn applications. They are usually applied with a special gun that fits on your garden hose, or a siphoning device. One teaspoonful to each gallon of water is the average amount recommended by most brands of soluble type plant foods. One pound makes 100 gallons of nutrient solution. Most guns made for soluble plant foods have a jar attached that will hold about a pound of concentrated plant food, and when ready to apply to the lawn the water mixes (or siphons) in correct proportion before it leaves the nozzle on the hose. Soluble plant foods have to be applied once every two or three weeks during the growing season. They are quick boosters and give wonderful color if used regularly. Some lawn experts use this type as a starter, but they still provide a good organic foundation for the long lasting plant food elements. Soluble PERFECT PLANT FOOD and NUTRI-SOL are both good for gun application.

WATERING AND MOWING

Sandy soils naturally require more watering than clay or low damp types. One rule of watering is to let your lawn show a mere sign of wilt, then give enough water to soak at least 6 inches or more. Don't apply the water any faster than the soil can take it up, and avoid light waterings frequently. Remember that Centipede grass needs very little water, but even if it looks wilted it can be revived by a good soaking.

* * *

Mowing is important, and it varies with the types of lawn grasses. Cool season grasses should be cut to a height of about 2 inches. Warm season types like Bermuda should be cut frequently and kept at 5/8 of an inch to keep good turf quality. Others like Zoysia, Centipedegrass, Carpet and St. Augustinegrass should be mowed to one inch in height. Some of the Bahia grasses become stubble-like if mowed too short, so it is best to give more frequent mowings than to allow grass to become tall.

Hibiscus

THE HIBISCUS reigns supreme among the flowering shrubs of the tropics. In recent years many new hybrids have appeared and are being used in the landscape designs of modern homes, gardens, estates, highways and parks. Because of the interest in this popular shrub, many communities have organized societies and study groups which has helped to establish the proper names and classifications of the older standard varieties and the newer hybrids. The named varieties available today run into many hundreds.

Single Red Hibiscus. Most common. but one of the hardiest.

the general characteristics of this group resemble those of the mallow. (See Hibiscus Relatives)

Many hibiscus species from China, East Africa and other parts of the world have played a part in the creation of new hybrids. The single scarlet red flowering hibiscus (perhaps the most common of all) is said to have come from China originally. Anyway its botanical name *Hibiscus rose-chinensis, or sinensis L* indicates the fact. The single red is still one of the most prolific, and dependable. It has been used extensively in planting hedges, fence rows, and in general landscape. The pollen from its flowers figures in many of the hybrids on the market. Otherwise it has been used as a parent plant. Another single red hibiscus species

BETTY HENDRY — Double Yellow No. 40.

The HIBISCUS is just one genus of more than 80 genera and is a member of the large MALLOW (*or Malvaceae*) family. Several of the members of this family such as the Althea, and the common roadside mallows have been used extensively in "crossing or hybridizing" to obtain new colors, shapes and patterns in the blossoms, and variations in the foliage. You may find hybrids with just about every color except blue or black, however a trace of blue has shown up recently in some new introductions. Even a color classified as "gunmetal" is among the hybrids of the last ten years. The purples, lavenders, or lilac colors were obtained by crossing and re-crossing with the various altheas having these colors.

Blossoms are large as a dinner plate may be found among the Hibiscus-Mallow crosses known as the Henderson cross which is sometimes termed the perennial hibiscus because they die back in the Fall and come back again in the early Spring. Although their blossoms are hibiscus-like,

PSYCHE — Brilliant red Schizopetalus type hibiscus

Hibiscus

from East Africa known as *Hibiscus schizopetalus* has played an important part in obtaining new blossom and foliage characteristics. Its flowers (2 to 3 inches) resemble small Japanese lanterns. The name *"schizopetalus"* means split petals. The name "fringed-hibiscus" is used by some to indicate Hibiscus *schizopetalus* and some of its hybrids, which include the red or white La France (now named Dainty), Psyche, Red Hawaiian, Sal-

VELVET TOUCH — One of the improved single red hibiscus; red and white color mixture.

mon Hawaiian and the extremely hardy and prolific large-flowered type called ROWENA WEDDING.

* * * *

Besides the numerous colors and variegations found in the many hundreds of named and unnamed varieties, there are also many variations in blossom shapes and in the foliage. Flower petals range from narrow to wide bases, some have loose petals with scalloped edges, others are crepey textured, ruffled, fluted, crested, over-lapped edges, reflexed, etc. Most growers and authorities classify blossoms as being either single, double, semi-double or crested. They are also classified as being one of the following shapes:

1. Saucer or salver-formed. This represents the largest majority of singles, such as the single red, single orange or salmon, Velvet Touch and others.
2. Recurved petals with wavy or scalloped edges as found on the Schizopetalus types mentioned.
3. Funnel-shaped flowers until they wilt, such as the Ruth Wynn Perry, or Glorious B or C.

Some varieties of hibiscus have a longer blooming period than others, and it is possible to have blooms almost all year round in such areas as Central and South Florida.

The older standards such as the Single Red, Double Red (Lamberti), Painted Lady, Versicolor, Dainty and others will grow and bloom under many adverse weather and soil conditions. Some of the newer hybrids are also hardy enough to be included, but some too are classified as being very touchy, except under ideal conditions. Sometimes an extreme cold spell will set back the hardiest of hibiscus and cause a delay in blooming the next year. Even some of the double-flowered types will put out single blossoms for a spell, or you may have dwarf flowers. In lower Central and South Florida you can usually expect two blooming periods from the majority of hibiscus. Normally these two periods are from April thru June, and September thru December.

* * * *

The more hardier types of hibiscus (old standards especially) will grow on a wide variety of soils, such as sand, muck, rockland or marl, however fairly rich soil will produce healthier looking plants. Plenty of moisture and sufficient plant food are among the requirements for best results. Where you have considerable rain fall during the year, it is possible to get fair results in the more sandy areas. It is best however to add organic materials, compost, peat, or manures whenever possible. If you live at the beach or where you have very sandy soil, it is a good policy to add about 5 lbs. of Colloidal Phosphate to the planting hole of each plant. Mix it with some organic matter like rotted leaves, compost, etc., and good top soil. Don't forget that mulching is a big help in retaining moisture and plant foods. Of course you will find various opinions about what is best to use for fertilizing hibiscus, but you can generally depend on almost any reliable brand of rose

HIBISCUS — Betty James

fertilizer applied once a month from March thru June. If you want extraordinary results, use a soluble plant food such as PERFECT HIBISCUS SPECIAL.

The most popular way to propagate Hibiscus is by cuttings, using softwood or tip cuttings of half-ripened wood taken from May thru July. Almost any of the rooting-mediums mentioned (under the Propagation of Plants chapter) may be used for your cuttings. The commercial growers use the Constant Mist method or the Air-Layering method. If you want to produce large plants in a hurry, then the Air-Layering method is best. Of course this means you have to have fairly large plants as stock, in order to take off a large limb with a well-formed top.

WE ARE RELATIVES OF THE HIBISCUS
HIBISCUS MUTABILIS

Many call me the CONFEDERATE ROSE, and some insist on calling me COTTONROSE. Botanist call me *Hibiscus mutabilis* (which means changeable). Anyway I do open my flowers white or pale pink in the morning and later in the day I have turned to dark pink. I have rather large leaves (3 to 5 lobes) with tomentose (that means

CONFEDERATE ROSE (*Hibiscus Mutabilis*) Opens white to pale pink in morning. Turns dark pink later in day.

fuzzy, furry, woolly, or sometimes velvety) on the underside. I am not too touchy either, as I will grow almost anywhere in Florida and even in some warm states. Just cut off a piece of my stem and treat it with hormone powder and stick me in the ground where I can get a little moisture and I will take root easily. I am a "cinch" in them fancy rooting mediums. Somebody crossed me up years ago, and now I have a double-flowered competitor.

HIBISCUS MOSCHEUTOS

I am just a common roadside mallow, so they say, but you know I am just as pretty as most of my relatives, and not near as touchy as some of them. Some call me an annual, some a perennial,

COMMON MALLOW

and that all depends where I grow and how, but one thing is certain, if you don't destroy my seeds, I'll be back next year. What about my flowers? Well some say we are rose, pink, or whitish, and others say I have been mixed up with another mallow and have yellow flowers with a red-eye, or again I am not really *Moscheutos* but have the name *Abelmoschus* (a musk-mallow). I'll tell you one thing, I am sort of sticky with that tomentose stuff on the underside of my leaves and along the stems and branches. All in all—there sure is a lot of us Common Mallows, but that guy Henderson in California used us to get those big fancy flowered plants he calls Hibiscus-Mallows.

HIBISCUS-MALLOWS

Well, they call me a Hibiscus-Mallow crossbreed, but I sure do stop the traffic when I am blooming during the summer months in Florida and Georgia and even as far north as Michigan. I must have more mallow blood than hibiscus, for like them I fold up during the winter months, and if you leave me in the ground in the warmer climates, or in containers elsewhere, I will make a comeback in the Spring.

My foliage is either like a hibiscus or a mallow, or betwixt the two. Cut out my dead wood in November or December and leave me alone, is all that I ask. Yes, I have several color combinations and flower patterns, and each with a name Mr. Henderson gave me, I think. Who's Mr. Henderson? Well he's the guy who runs the Henderson Experimental Gardens in Fresno, Cal., and the one who crossed me and caused all this commotion. One named Brilliant Cerise has a huge flower with

Hibiscus

a cerise color naturally. Super Rose another large flower about 10 inches across, is a beautiful satin-pink color. White Beauty too has 10-inch flowers. A number of other Hibiscus-Mallows have flowers ranging from 5 to 8 inches across. Mr. Geo. Riegel of The Riegel Plant Co. of Experiment, Ga. has even crossed some of the others, (the double-crosser), and has obtained some striking color combinations. Anyway, Mr. Riegel has done a lot towards publicizing (he sells them too) the Hibiscus-Mallows in the South and other states.

What about seeds? Well, some of them set seeds without any aid from man, but others do require hand pollination. I take pollen from most all the mallows, and at times from certain hibiscus and altheas. If you get seeds to form, they will keep for long periods, but it is best to plant them about January or February, however they seem to thrive, no matter when you plant them. If planted in Fall, they may come up and grow a little, then die back for a spell and then come back to life in the Spring. If you plant me in the Northern states, put me in large kegs or other containers, and when cold weather comes, move me into the basement or garage, until signs of Spring appear.

HIBISCUS SABDARIFFA

My name is a mouthful, and I am better known in many parts of the world as ROSELLE (or Rozelle), and some call me the Jamaica or Red (also White) Sorrel. In Florida the old-timers call me the Florida Cranberry Bush, because of the sauce they make out of my pods (calyces) that is a good substitute for Cranberry Sauce. Whatever you call me, I am a useful hibiscus relative to certain people, and for certain purposes, and believe it or not I am grown commercially in many areas. My flower sepals or calyces are called "accrescent" or in other words I continue to grow and become a pod resembling a short okra pod. If not allowed to dry out they are succulent, and in this stage they are removed to make either sauce, jelly, or even pickles. Delightful ades and drinks are made from the concentrated jelly-like substance.

Some people argue that I am a red hibiscus, but let me tell you, I have several variations. The true Roselle of commerce has reddish stems, leaves and fruits and is a native of the West Indies, and is actually a green and red mixture, with perhaps more green than red. The green form which is known as "White Sorrel" bears greenish-white fruits, but because they are not as acid as the more reddish roselle, it is not advisable to plant them for jelly or sauce uses. The true roselle flowers are yellow with a red-eye. There is a red-flower with red leaves and stems found on a very common bush in Florida that is often mistaken for the ROSELLE.

The ROSELLE is classified as an annual shrub that reaches from 6 to 8 feet in height. It is started from seed which is planted in open ground, or rows spaced 5 to 6 feet apart. Plants should be thinned to 2½ feet apart in the rows. In Florida it is best to plant in March or April. One packet of seed will plant about 25 feet of row. It takes about 175 days from seed to maturity. Seed may be obtained from Kilgore Seed Co. in Plant City, or Miami, Fla., or from the Crenshaw--McMichael Seed Co. of Tampa, Fla., and from many local seed stores.

The red leaf, stalk and flower hibiscus often mistaken for roselle. (*Hib. eetveldeanus*)

HIBISCUS SYRIACUS
The Shrub Althea

As a shrub I produce flowers so beautiful that I have a name associated with the Holy Land and Scriptures and for that reason I am called the ROSE OF SHARON. In the northern parts of Florida and in most of the Gulf States, plus those along the Atlantic Coast as far north as North Carolina they call me by the simple name of ALTHEA or botanically *Althea syriacus*. Some call me the Shrub Althea to distinguish me from another Althea (in the Malaviscus group) which is better known as Hollyhocks.

The Shrub Althea does well in the cooler areas, and where there is considerable clay in the soil. In Central and South Florida it will grow in shady or semi-shady areas, but seldom lasts very long. The regular Hibiscus offers it too much competition in these areas.

Altheas often attain the height of 12 feet, however most of them average from 5 to 8 feet. Their leaves are 3-lobed and are generally toothed, and a fairly dark green color. The flowers range from white to pink, rose to purple and some even have a bluish cast. There are numerous hybrids available, some with single or double flowers. Mark Riegel, whom we mentioned before, has produced a number of excellent ALTHEAS with new color combinations, such as the KREIDER BLUE (double) with 3 to 4 inch blossoms, PINK DELIGHT a double light flesh Pink, COLIE MULLINS a double wine red, BETTY KURZ a semi-double wine red with deeper red center, and for a pure white with large snowy blossoms 3 to 4 inches wide, I recommend EFFIE RIEGEL.

HIBISCUS ESCULENTUS (OKRA)

My that's a big name for the vegetable hibiscus which is better known as OKRA. Like the Roselle my blossoms form into pods that range from 2 inches on up to 8 inches, and when they cook me some people think I am really slick. Many Florida and Georgia "Crackers" slice my pods crosswise into little wheels and fry me in corn meal and boy is that good. Out there in Louisiana the Creoles and natives call me GUMBO and they keep me in the soup. Even Heinz and Campbell put me in their soup they call Gumbo Soup, and they are wise, for you can't beat me for flavoring. People with ulcerated stomachs should know more about me, for when I am boiled and consumed, I can help soothe those intestinal linings. Another way I can help is by using my powdered form known as Okra tablets (also called Vege-Mucin) and usually sold by Health Food Stores and some drug stores.

OKRA (*Hibiscus Esculentus*)

Okra is a favorite garden vegetable not only in Florida but in many Southern states. In Florida it is a major vegetable crop and can be planted in almost every section of the state. In North Florida the planting time is March thru May, and again in August for early fall crops. In Central and South Florida the planting time is from Feb-

ruary thru early April, and again in September into October. It requires from 40 to 60 days to harvest. It is best to remove pods when full and when they are tender. If allowed to grow they may become tough.

Okra does best on sandy loam soils with good drainage, and with a fair amount of fertility. Plant in rows 3 to 4 feet apart with about 3 feet between plants. Some growers advise cutting pods from plant every second day in order to obtain tender pods for home consumption or soups.

There are a number of improved varieties recommended: Perkins Spineless (53 days) with practically spineless pods, also, an old standby, the Perkins Long Green, and a very fine semi-dwarf variety is the Clemson Spineless (55 days) which produces thick, uniform, straight and large ridged pods. This variety reaches to 4½ feet on fairly good soil.

Don't fail to plant at least a few Okra bushes for good food and a great help to the health. Learn to like it, if on first try you don't.

HIBISCUS TILIACEUS

All of my relatives can boast. I am the largest of the ones classified as Hibiscus. I am really a tree of huge proportions and sometimes I reach up to 75 feet in height. My leaves range from 3 to 10 times the size of ordinary hibiscus, and some of them take on beautiful shades of red, yellow, purple and other shades at certain times of the year. I have blossoms that look like many of those found on shrub type hibiscus, and I start off as a shade of yellow, then turn to orange shades, and finally to a deep maroon color, all within 24 hours. You will often find a mixture of colors of yellow, orange and maroon on a tree during a sunny day.

In some of the warm areas like Hawaii they often call me a MAHOE or Mahoe Hibiscus tree, but in South and Central Florida they simply call me a TREE HIBISCUS or some say *Hibiscus tiliaceus* which is correct. Because I take on such huge trunks and limbs, a heavy wind may topple me over, especially if I am out in the open areas, so be sure and plant me where I have some protection if possible. Now, here is another suggestion, if you will prune off some of those heavy limbs every year, and keep me from getting too top-heavy, it will help considerably. Another thing, when you set out a small specimen, be sure and make a real deep hole, so that a good part of the base and trunk is down deep.

Where can I grow? Almost anywhere around water, fresh or salt, and in fairly moist ground from Pinellas County southward to the Keys, or from Vero Beach on the East Coast of Florida to the Keys.

Hibiscus

Blossoms of the Tree Hibiscus change from yellow, through orange to maroon in one day.

When you buy a Hibiscus Tree from a nursery, you may get quite a few variations in size of foliage, color of flowers, etc., because many of them have been crossed in some way, and they may have some of the blood of a close relative known as the CUBAN BAST or *Hibiscus elatus* whose flowers are mostly lemon yellow or sulphur yellow, but do not change color as in the *Hibiscus tiliaceus*. Some say the Cuban Bast has even greater stature than the Hibiscus Tree, but that is doubtful, however it is highly recommended and just as beautiful in form and foliage. One thing common to both trees, is that they are considered among the fastest growers, but be sure and allow them plenty of space to spread.

OTHER IMPORTANT HIBISCUS RELATIVES

TURK'S CAP

We have been considering the HIBISCUS as a family with many relatives, but according to the manner of botanical classification, it is just one genus of the large family called the *Malaviscus or Malvaceae*. Perhaps the best known plant in the group found in abundance in Florida is the one commonly called the TURK'S CAP or *Malaviscus grandiflorus*. The Chinese call it the sleeping hibiscus, because the drooping blossoms never open completely. They blossom so profusely, however, that they make a beautiful mass color effect. Although the red flowering Turk's Cap is the most common, there is also a pink variety, which sometimes has both red and pink on the same bush. Occasionally you will find blossoms that may be classified as white. They do vary with changes of weather.

If you will supply sufficient organic materials and fertilizer to the soil, your Turk's Cap will take on beautiful foliage and flower colors. Even though they grow with extreme neglect, you will be amply rewarded if you give them a little care. Be sure and prune them once or twice a year or even more if they seem to get out of bounds.

TURK'S CAP makes a beautiful hedge, border plant, or a background shrub. For a hedge, you can line out hardwood cuttings where they are to grow, and if the soil is not too sandy or dry, you will have a good hedge within 18 months. The cuttings placed in containers or beds under CONSTANT MIST will have roots like grandpa's whiskers in nothing flat.

There is another plant that is often called the Midget Turk's Cap, and its flowers are similar in shape and color, but an inch long with a protruding pistil with light purple pollen and deep red stamens. This plant is properly called *Achania Malaviscus*. Apply some of the pollen to the stamens and a seed pod that resembles a bright red cherry will form. The seeds can be planted to start more Achanias, or it is a simple matter to start them from cuttings. Seldom do you find this plant at nurseries, or find the seeds listed, so you may have to search among your garden friends or botanical gardens. They are more or less common in gardens of Florida, but very few people know their real name.

Charles James, Jr.—One of the most popular double hibiscus, base petals reddish-orange, centers are definitely five parted, mingled reddish orange and gold, tipped golden yellow.

Betty Chalk — Deep red single (hybrid) hibiscus. Throat deeper red, medium flowers, excellent foliage.

Single Butterfly (yellow)

Azaleas in Florida

AZALEAS ARE the highlight flowering shrubs of nearly all Southern gardens from the Carolinas to Lake Okeechobee in Florida. Their incomparable beauty and ornamental value is without a rival.

There is a long list of glorious varieties with single or double flowers, with colors ranging from pure white to the deepest and most glowing scarlet, crimsons, shades of lavender and purple, and numerous hybrids that are beautifully spotted and strangely marked. When in full bloom they are so floriferous that scarcely a leaf can be seen. Although there are many azaleas that start to bloom as early as October, the real color "en masse" season is February and March in Florida. This is the time that gardens like the famous Cypress Gardens of Winter Haven, and many others all over the state draw thousands of visitors to see the spectacular display. Many thousands of homes use azaleas in the driveway, along the sidewalks, in the garden or general landscape. Of the thousands grown, the largest majority is represented in two groups which are commonly called INDIAN (*Azalea indica*) and the KURUME (*Azalea Kurume or obtusum*). *Azalea indica* or the Indian azalea is supposed to have originated in India, but authorities tell us there are no azaleas in India, but somehow this name is firmly established in the minds of the general public. Some claim they are natives of China. The Kurume azaleas were originally imported from Japan about 1917. To further complicate the botanical confusion, it is now a fact (seemingly) that Azaleas are actually Rhododendrons (that is they are in that genus) and are a member of the family known as *Ericacae*, which includes many other acid-loving plants such as the Blueberry, Cranberry, Huckleberry, Arbutus and Leucothe. The shrubs we know as Azaleas are actually Rhododendrons with five stamens in each flower, while the ones commonly called Rhododendrons have ten stamens in each flower.

INDIAN AZALEAS

The so-called Indian azaleas are evergreen shrubs with large single or double flowers that sometimes measure as much as four inches across. Some are practically dwarf and slow-growing, while others grow rapidly into large shrubs. The various varieties on the market are the results of much crossing, and therefore not derived from a single species. Perhaps the most common of this group is the FORMOSA with its very large lilac-lavender flowers. This is a mid-season bloomer and very hardy. DUC DE ROHAN is another favorite and one of the most responsive of all the ever-

AZALEAS — Colorful gems of the Southern Gardens.

bloomers. Blooms profusely for long periods. Color is brilliant salmon orange on low compact bushes which have no equal for front row use. Plant them in groups of 10 or more. This variety will stand shearing. FIELDER'S WHITE is one of the popular early bloomers with pure white flowers. A very upright grower and the best of whites. GLORY OF SUNNING HILL is a popular midseason variety with large orange-scarlet flowers, and is a free-bloomer.

SOUTHERN CHARM with large clear pink flowers, a sport of Formosa variety is a strong grower and midseason bloomer. FISHER'S PINK also a midseason bloomer, but with lighter pink color is a very strong and compact bushy grower. For an good rosy salmon color, plant the DUKE OF WELLINGTON. There are several azaleas known as the Macrantha group and MACRANTHA PINK single, MACRANTHA PINK double, MACRANTHA ORANGE are all very hardy late bloomers and very compact growers. For an early orange color with medium-sized blooms plant the PRESIDENT CLAY. The tall brother of Duc De Rohan is one called LAWSAL. This very compact upright grower produces color masses of salmon-orange blooms 4½ to 7 ft. high. A vivid variegated variation of Duc is one called MRS. ENKE and is used to compliment the colors of the Duc and Lawsal. One of the finest variegated azaleas is the GEORGE LINDLEY TABER. It is soft lavender-pink that is faintly streaked darker pink and mottled cerise, also slightly fragrant. A fine cold resistant type, it blooms in March in North Florida. The PRIDE OF MOBILE should be in every plant-

Azaleas in Florida

ing, for this one is a cloud of rich watermelon-pink crisp 3-inch flowers that will be the pride of any garden or home. These are only some suggestions of good varieties to plant. There are many other very fine Indian Azaleas of equal quality or beauty. If you desire the giant type Azaleas for your plantings, then here are four of the very best ones for Florida: SNOWBALL with big double pure white blooms, TRIOMPHE a semi-double crimson, PINK LEOPARD with huge pink petals with white ruffled edges and leopard markings of lush red dots, ALBERT ELIZABETH with huge double white flowers which are frilled with pink edges, and has a soft lacey look.

KURUME AZALEAS

This group of azaleas are equal if not superior to the Indian varieties. The Kurumes are a solid mass of color when in bloom, and hide almost all their foliage. Colors are rich and varied and contain many new shades not represented in others. Although the Kurumes are of slower growth than Indian types, they make nice speci mens with very compact form, and equal almost all other evergreen shrubs in this respect. Even the small plants will bloom and each season as they increase in size they increase in beauty. Some of the popular ones for Florida planting include the HINODEGIRI one of the most brilliant of all dwarf azaleas. A very shapely plant with evergreen foliage and fiery red blooms. Ideal for low hedge and may be used as a pot-plant. HEBE, a deep red or scarlet, for midseason hose-in-hose type blooms. CHRISTMAS CHEER another hose-in-hose type bloomer with Christmas red color. For pink the COREL BELLS is a profuse midseason bloomer with hose-in-hose blooms of dainty shell-pink. APPLE BLOSSOMS with apple-blossom pink blooms and glossy green foliage is very compact and hardy. SWEETHEART SUPREME produces hose-in-hose type blooms with a blush pink color that resemble a sweetheart rose. It is very compact and has dark green foliage.

For a good white plant, SNOW is a free-flowering pure white Kurume with very glossy green foliage, and compact form. For a peach color plant, the PEACH BLOW. For lavenders use either LAVENDER QUEEN or CATTLEYA.

SUCCESS WITH AZALEAS

First of all, it must be understood that Azaleas belong to a special group of plants known as extreme acid-loving types. This means they do not like alkaline or sweet soils. The soil must be lime-free, and must contain lots of organic matter. Soil scientists state that all plant life has a preference within a certain acid-alkaline ratio, and this is referred to as the "ph" of the soil. Azaleas, Camellias and Gardenias, prefer a ph of 4.5 to 5.3—so the first step to success with these plants is to get your soil in the proper ph range. Soil testing kits are sold by most garden stores or nurseries which makes it an easy matter to determine the exact ph of your azalea soil. You can skip all this testing and trust to luck, provided you supply the beds with sufficient amounts of decayed and rotted leaves, sawdust, peat, and vegetative matter, plus about half or 50% good rich top soil. Perhaps the most widely used combination is leaf mold and peat moss well mixed. Next best bet is to buy a good ready-mixed compost. Some further suggestions regarding organic matter is to use rotten wood, or bark from old logs or stumps, mix in some old sawdust (cypress is best) and oak leaves. The "just-right" azalea bed is one that is light and friable, which never should become pasty or stiff — nor should it harden in dry weather.

By all means use a MULCH. This is important to conserve moisture and to protect the shallow roots from the sun. Mulches help keep down the weeds. Any weeds that appear should be pulled up.

Azaleas like plenty of water at times, but they do not like wet feet. This means that good drainage should be provided. During dry weather, give a thorough soaking every 10 days, this is better than frequent light sprinklings. Syringe the tops on newly set plants or old well established plants. This is in addition to the regular waterings. Azaleas require more water when in bloom than at any other time, in fact they require almost twice the amount of water to make them happy. You can apply large amounts of water to the tops when they are in flower. Be sure your water is lime-free. Lime injury manifests itself in the foliage. In the earlier stages the veins may still be green, but the spaces between are yellowish and have a mottled appearance. If this continues the leaves drop and twigs will die back.

If there is too much lime or alkalinity (apparent by the foliage and twigs) then here is a suggested treatment — scatter aluminum sulphate over the bed at the rate of $1/4$ to $1/2$ lb. per square yard. Spread it thinly around the plants, or better still mix with peat moss or muck.

Azaleas in Florida

HOW MUCH FERTILIZER?

When using one of the special Azalea-Camellia formulas of reliable brands, the usual feeding schedule is as follows: for the first spring feeding (that follows the blooming season) use approximately one pound of fertilizer for each 25 square feet of bed. Six weeks later another feeding should follow using the same amount. For single plants the amount is usually from ¼ to ½ pound, depending on the size of plant. An alternate feeding schedule that is very effective is to reduce the total amount of fertilizer to be used into four equal parts and apply every two weeks. Starting in April (in most areas of Florida) this will bring the last feeding to the middle of May. All feeding should be stopped in order to allow the plants to go into their summer rest period . . . and to help set a good crop of buds, which in turn helps reduce the tendency of azaleas to make dangerously late fall growth.

CONTROL OF INSECTS, DISEASES AND PESTS

Red spider and scale are two of the most troublesome insect pests. Mealy bug and white flies are a nuisance at times. Then there is flower blight which is sometimes very serious in cool foggy weather. If dried-up flowers appear, it is best to remove them along with mulch underneath and burn them. Flower blight may be controlled by spraying Zineb about three times a week while the flowers are opening. Leaf galls occur sometimes, and they should be hand-picked and burned. If this condition is heavy, then use a low lime Bordeaux mixture (6-2-100).

SPRAY SCHEDULE FOR AZALEAS

1. In Spring — just after blooming:

   (a) White-oil emulsion—such as
   Florida Volck, 1 gal. to 100 gals. water.
   Powdered derris 1½ lbs. Black Leaf 40.

   (b) For Dusts use such items as
   END-O-PEST

   (c) Prepared formulas such as OILAN
   and others may be used instead of
   other above items.
   Pests: Lacebug - Thrips - Mites (Spider)

2. Last of May or first of June:
   Spray: Same as above.
   Pests: Mealybug, Lacebug, Thrips, Red Spider and Peony scale.

3. Last of September:
   Spray: Same as above.
   Pests: All pests above.

PROPAGATION OF AZALEAS

Azaleas may be rooted from cuttings taken from the last of April until August. Tip cuttings are best, and should be about 3 to 4 inches long with a few leaves left on upper portion. Treat each cutting with a root inducing compound such as Naph, Rootone, etc. Place them in any of the mediums mentioned in chapter on Propagation and place under misting device if possible. Sharp builders sand or perlite may be used and covered with cheesecloth for a period. Be sure either mixture is not allowed to dry out.

Air layering is used to make larger bushes in a short time. Sometimes this method is referred to as marcottage. (See section on Air-layering). Still another way to start fair sized plants in a hurry is to pull down the lower branches of a growing plant, so that they touch the soil and cover with soil for two or three inches. Make a slit on the underside of limb before covering with soil. This will cause roots to form at this point. If necessary the limbs may be pegged down or held in place with a stone or brick. After a few months the new plant can be separated from the old and transplanted.

* * * *

FURTHER NOTES ON AZALEAS

Do not at any time use a hoe or other instrument to cultivate around the roots of Azaleas. They are surface feeders and will not stand cultivation. Mulch is the answer.

* * * *

Balled or burlapped plants from nurseries can be moved at any time, however it is best to avoid periods of full flush of growth. A good time is just before or during the flowering period.

* * * *

Wonderful azaleas can be grown with soluble plant foods. Try experimenting with single plants and note how fast they grow. Feedings are of course more frequent, because all elements are soluble and fast acting. Some like to use both types of plant foods, that is the dry formulas and the soluble types. Liquid types too may be used.

* * * *

Azaleas will grow in sun, but certain ones like filtered sunlight. Many parks all over the state use them along the sidewalks and pathways where there is both sunlight and partial shade.

* * * *

PERFCT 100% soluble Azalea Plant Food — is highly recommended for azaleas, camellias, or Gardenias.

Camellias in Florida

IN THE DEEP SOUTH, the natives and many of the old timers place the Camellia among the so-called romantic flowering shrubs which include Jasmines, Gardenias, Tea Roses and Azaleas. For many generations they were simply called "JAPONICAS", and little did they realize that the word meant Japan and it was actually a part of the full botanical name of *Camellia japonica*. Not until recent years did you have to draw any distinction between Japonica and Sasanqua types of Camellias, each is different yet both belong to the Tea or Thea family. Southerners in general pronounce Camellias as Ca-meel-ias, while perfectionists and others insist on calling them Ca-mell-ias. The Latin name was in honor of a Moravian botanist named George Joseph Kamel, so with a capital C or a short e or long e sound . . . well . . . they are simply beautiful.

Camellia japonicas are evergreen shrubs with leathery deep green glossy foliage. They grow in many shapes from compact globose, to tall columnar upright specimens. There are some with irregular shapes, and others with spreading habits. Some are considered as slow growers, others are classified from medium to rapid. Certain ones will reach from 15 to 35 feet in time, and take on tree like proportions.

There certainly is a variety of flower shapes to be had in the long list of named varieties on the market today. Some are single, others are semi-double, irregular double, imbricated double, and further classifications state they are carnation-like, rose-like, and even marbleized. Some do have an artificial appearance. With the various colors of white, pink and red in so many patterns and markings you have exquisite beauty for any home or garden.

PLANTING FOR A PURPOSE

The majority of Camellia japonicas requires medium to light shade conditions, otherwise they will have that sun-burned appearance. Certain varieties will stand the full sun of northern Florida, but in lower areas it is best to utilize the light shade of trees, tall shrubs or a lattice trellis. Of the thousands of named varieties found in nurseries and catalogs, it is possible to select types suitable for any garden, home or landscape location. Keep in mind that many hundreds of Camellias are classified as Standards, and many more as either Rare Camellias or Extremely Rare varieties. It is best to stick to the Standards if you are a beginner at growing Camellias. When a so-called Rare Camellia is on the market for at least 10 years, it may be classified as a Standard, so it is not unusual to find them classified differently in various catalogs.

Camellia Mathotiana Rubra

Let us consider the doorway of your home as the first example in planting. A tall pillar type Camellia such as the Professor C. S. Sargent would be ideal. It bears solid crimson colored blossoms with a thick peony form (called irregular double). It is a rapid upright grower and considered an early-to-midseason bloomer. Another choice would be Elena Nobile with its small deep rose-pink fully imbricated blossoms. If you want a heavy mass effect at the corner of the house then plant Aunt Jetty, Hermes, Pink Perfection, or Mathotiana. If you have high windows on any side that is semi-shady then plant Donckelaari, Elegans Variegated, Prince Eugene Napoleon or Magnoliaeflora. For large expanses of unbroken masonry plant the spreading Lady Clare, Elegans Pink, or Gigantea. For neutral fillers under windows, by screen porches, patios, etc. you may use any of the globose or compact types, such as Alba Plena (white), White Empress, Debutante (pink), Victor Emmanuel (red).

For private outdoor areas, it is best to plant small flowering trees, tall shrubs, or hardy evergreen-shrubs of the broadleaf types in the background and then set your camellias in front. Some of the deciduous trees (those who lose their leaves) such as the redbud, dogwood, mimosa, Jerusalem Thorn (Parkinsonia) are useful for this purpose. They provide light shade during the Camellia season.

Nearly all types of Camellias may be used for a boundary or fence line. Some use the tall upright growers in back or center and the low-growing types on either side. Another favorite way to use Camellias is to plant tall or upright types under the outer spread of Live Oak trees or other large trees that provide some filtered sunlight.

Camellias in Florida

Camellia Sasanqua Rosea

RECOMMENDED VARIETIES FOR FLORIDA

The following is a list of easy to grow camellias suitable for most of Florida as far south as the Everglades. WHITE: Alba Plena, White Empress, Purity. LIGHT PINK: Debutante, Pink Perfection, Rose Dawn, Laurel Leaf. DARK PINK: Lady Clare, Elegans Pink, Rose Dawn, RED: Chandleri E l e g a n s, Mathiotiana, Kimberly, Prof. C. S. Sargent, Victor Emmanuel, Prince Eugene Napoleon, Scarlett O'Hara, Daikagura. VARIEGATED: Elegans Var., Governor Moulton, Adolphe Audusson Var., Gigantea, Sweet Pea, C. M. Hovey.

* * * *

For catalogs of varieties: Holmes Nurseries, P. O. Box 417, Tampa, Fla., Thomasville Nurseries, Inc. Thomasville, Ga., National Nurseries, Biloxi, Miss., Glen Saint Mary Nurseries, Glen Saint Mary, Fla.

CAMELLIA PLANTING

Camellia japonicas require acid conditions, with the ideal soil being in the range of ph 5.0 to 6.0. Like Azaleas, they thrive best in soil that is at least 50% humus by volume. The sites selected to plant your camellias should be well drained and lightly shaded.

Prepare a hole twice as big as the ball of earth on each plant. Mix the best of the topsoil removed with an equal amount of peat humus or peat moss. To a bushel of this prepared soil add about two quarts of dried sheep manure and a cupful of a good Azalea-Camellia Special fertilizer. Return part of the mixture to the hole and tamp down well so it is firm and solid. Set the balled plant

on this foundation; it should be high enough so the nursery soil line is a trifle higher than the surrounding ground; this allows for some settling later. Be sure no hollow air space is left under the ball to hold water and rot-off new roots.

Fill in around the ball with the rest of the prepared soil. Several times during this filling in, let water from the hose run gently in the hole to force out air pockets, and settle the dirt. After it is filled and firmed down to the level of surrounding ground a rim of dirt may be pulled up to make a saucer to hold water. Do not water again until the surface soil is dry. A good soaking once a week does more good than daily sprinkling.

Camellias planted in good soil with plenty of humus should not need any commercial fertilizer the first year. After that fertilize each year in February and April with special Azalea-Camellia fertilizer.

After the camellias are well established, avoid frequent watering—so the roots will go deep where soil moisture is constant. A deep rooted plant suffers less drought damage than the plant which has formed many fine feeder roots near the surface.

* * * *

Camellias are spaced according to their growth habits, size and form. Space the average at least 5 to 6 feet or more apart. Some of the extra large or tall ones may need 10 to 15 feet of spacing between plants.

* * * *

Mulching is worthwhile for Camellias. Many types of materials can be used for this purpose, and it includes pine straw, shredded cypress bark, pine bark, peanut hulls, cane bagasse, straw, leaves, sawdust or sawdust-peat mixtures, water hyacinths (dried), pods of Mothers Tongue tree (Albizzia lebbek), and peat. If sawdust or shaving are used additional nitrogen will be required. Castor pomace, and milorganite can be used effectively.

PEST CONTROL

Camellia dieback or twig blight is probably the worst enemy of Camellias in Florida. To help prevent the spread of the disease, cut out branches that wilt and die back and burn them immediately. For control use the Bordeaux mixture. Other pests and disease include scales such as Florida Red, Camellia and Tea scale. Recommended controls include 50% emulsion Malathion. oil emulsion, and many similar products. Suggest you get in touch with your local dealer—or write to the Agricultural Extension Service in Gainesville, Fla. and request mimeograph bulletin called "CAMELLIA GROWING" by E. W. McElwee. This gives outlined measure of insect control.

Red spider mite, leaf eating beetles, climbing cut-worms, grasshoppers and katydids can be controlled with prepared products such as END-O-PEST, ISOTOX GARDEN SPRAY, Florida VOLCK Paste Emulsion, BOTANO Garden Dust, and other similar products.

Camellias in Florida

SASANQUA CAMELLIAS

The Sasanqua Camellia bears smaller flowers which are hardier and more graceful than the better known and larger Japonicas. They bloom when the plants are quite small, and therefore are well adapted for growing in pots, tubs, and other containers suitable for the patio. Outdoors they are not as touchy as the Japonicas, for they will grow in full sun and in various soils without requiring extreme acid conditions. Their rich green elliptic leaves measure from one to three inches and have finely scalloped margins. With their small leaves and slender branchlets, plus the arching and open habits of growth, the Sasanqua creates a different effect in the garden or landscape than the heavier specimens of the Japonicas.

The single flowered Sasanquas produce blooms that are reminiscent of the wild roses. Although there are more singles than other types, a good selection of doubles or semi-doubles may be obtained. It is claimed that over 100 varieties have been introduced from Japan in recent years, and include pinks, rose red, purplish reds and white. Individual flowers measure from one to three inches across, and have from five to nine petals which are usually crisped or wavy towards the apex.

In Florida the Sasanquas start blooming as early as September and last until February, sometimes overlapping the Japonicas which start as early as December or January. Many local nurseries and catalog firms offer the following standard Sasanqua Camellias.

SASANQUA CAMELLIA VARIETIES

APPLE BLOSSOM—Single with fairly large white flowers tinged with pink. Very fast growing and usually the first to flower.

ROSEA—Medium single flower type.

CLEOPATRA—Large deep pink flowers that are semi-double, and with crinkled petals.

Sasanque Camellia Oleifera

Leaf and buds of Camellia Sasanqua

OLEIFERA—Large pink flowers with crinkled petals. White tipped with rose.

SNOW - ON - THE - MOUNTAIN—Large double carnation-like white flowers. There is a pink flowered one called PINK SNOW.

SETSUGEKKA — Very large semi-double with faint pink tinge, and ruffled edges.

SHOWA-NO-SAKAE—Also known as USU-BENI. One of the newer varieties of doubles with soft pink color. Upright vigorous bush with good foliage.

HINODEGUMO — Semi-double blush-pink with deeper edges. Said to be the most beautiful of all Sasanquas.

TANYA—Small narrow and sharp pointed foliage. Small single flowered blooms that are delicately sweet-scented and of Bengal-rose hue.

MINO-NO-YUKI—Semi-double pure white with golden stamens.

HEBE—Single, phlox-pink flowers freely produced. Upright open plant.

BRIAR ROSE—Soft clear pink like a wild rose. Small dark green foliage.

BLANCHETTE—Single white flowers tinted on margins, reminding you of dogwood blossoms. Very sturdy and upright, with dainty green foliage.

Roses for Florida

THERE ARE many classifications of roses however the average gardener is not concerned ordinarily to which one a rose belongs, as he or she is about their beauty of form, color, fragrance and ability to produce a quantity of buds and blooms without too much effort. This is of course a big order, and seldom do we get so much without considerable effort, however there is one classification that comes close, which is the group that is known as "old-fashioned" tea roses. They are actually the roses of yesterday, or you might call them the roses of Grandmother's day.

THE OLD FASHIONED TEA ROSES

Old rose books state that the original tea rose was known botanically as Rosa odorata and that they came from China. It further states that the tea rose is a slender growing bush, branching freely and with smooth bark, shiny, but never rough or hairy. Young growths are often copper colored and prickles are less abundant than most roses, and often completely absent on some. Perhaps the reason they were called "tea roses" was the tea scent. Then again it might be that because they came from China there was a tea association in some manner. Anyway there is a range of colors from almost white to darker red shades. Tea roses are part of the romance of the "Old South" as much as camellias, gardenias and magnolias. Even today you will find many growing around older homes of cities and small towns. There is one in Florida that the natives call the "Cracker Rose," however its correct name is LOUIS PHILLIPE, and is a very prolific bearer of medium sized deep red blooms. Freshly opened blossoms may be cut, but seldom last longer than a day. This is mainly a landscape rose which seems to thrive under the most adverse conditions

Old Fashioned Tea Rose — Gross an Teplitz

and even without attention. With attention however, it takes on better color in foliage and produces many more flowers. It starts easily from cuttings. Many nurseries all over the state have Louis Phillipe roses in cans.

* * * *

Mr. Sam Hjort who with his family operates the Thomasville Nurseries, Inc., in Thomasville, Georgia, has specialized in growing old-fashioned tea roses for years, and his catalog (which also has all the newer roses) lists some of the very best for Florida and South Georgia climate. The following are some of his recommendations:

BARONESS HENRIETTE SNOW: with pointed buds and well formed double flowers of peach pink. WM. R. SMITH: a large double-flowered type with long lasting bluish-pink blossoms on stiff stems — excellent for cut flowers. MAMAN COCHET: a clear silvery pink with long pointed buds, large fragrant blossoms, excellent for cut flowers. MADAME LOMBARD: a rank grower that produces carmine-pink flowers shaded with salmon, and turns to red when in full glory.

MRS. DUDLEY CROSS: a vigorous yellow rose when opening, but gradually develops tints of pink. Place one of these roses alongside the famous PEACE Rose and it is hard to tell the difference. DUCHESS DE BRABANT: a very hardy and vigorous tea rose and one of the real favorites. Not a cutting type rose, but does produce an abundance of soft shell-pink flowers on short stems. They are globular in shape when fully opened.

Old Fashioned Tea Rose — Baroness Henriette Snow.

Roses for Florida

The old-fashioned tea roses resist blackspot (bugaboo of most roses in existence) better than the majority of other types. They seldom have as many thorns as the newer tea roses or other hybrids. Not all old roses are classified as tea roses. Many of the old roses were commonly cal'ed Ramblers, Baby Ramblers, Sweetheart or Fairy Roses, Everblooming roses and many more localized names. Some of the old roses were actually members of a group known as Polyanthas which bore many clusters of flowers, mainly used for color and mass flowering effects. CECILE BRUNNER is really the SWEETHEART ROSE of yesterday. It is a Polyantha-tea cross.

FLORIBUNDA ROSES

Crossing the Polyanthas with the modern tea rose produced a group that is now known as the FLORIBUNDA rose. This group has the best qualities and characteristics of both parents. Their flowers usually appear in clusters, however many fine hybrids now on the market produce many single flowers on long stems suitable for cutting roses. Some actually have both clusters and single flowers on the same bush. One such rose called the FASHION has the distinction of being the only rose to win six International Awards. Credit goes to hybridizer Eugene Boerner and the Jackson-Perkins Co. of Newark, N. Y. This rose started a new vogue in color with its Oriental-red buds which change to a luminous coral suffused with gold when open. There is now an IVORY FASHION that makes a good addition to the long list of Floribundas. Not all Floribundas have large flowers, for instance the one called THE FAIRY produces hundreds of shell-pink roses ranging in size from a quarter to a fifty cent piece. Its pretty boxwood-like foliage is shiny and bright green, and almost touches the ground on a fully developed bush. Bushes average 2 to 3 ft. high, but may attain 4 feet. The Fairy Rose blooms from late March up to the cold weather and thrives without much care. Among the older favorites in this classification are the FLORADORA, POULSEN'S BEDDER, and single flowered BETTY PRIOR and DONALD PRIOR which remind you of Dogwood blossoms.

* * * *

Some of the well known Floribundas offered by rose firms and local nurseries include the following: Fashion, Ivory Fashion, Circus, Moonsprite, Wildfire, Fanfare, Spartan, S u m m e r Snow, Jiminy Cricket, Geranium Red, Gold Cup, Red Ruffles, Amy Vanderbilt, Red Pinocchio, Lavender Pinocchio, Ma Perkins, Fusilier, Flameburst, Capri, Golden Fleece. Many more are advertised in flower and garden magazines, housekeeping and farm magazines.

HYBRID TEA ROSES

HYBRID TEA ROSES constitute the largest majority of roses grown all over the world. They are often referred to as "Patented Roses" and when the patent runs out they are usually called "Standard Hybrid Tea Roses." Hybrid Tea Roses are crosses between old fashioned teas, hybrid perpetuals and virtually all other classes. Most of the cut roses sold on the flower market are from hybrid tea bushes, however the muchly improved Floribunda roses are coming to the front and offering much competition. There are so many new roses of both the hybrid teas, and floribundas it is like trying to pick a necktie from a large assortment. One thing to keep in mind when buying a brand new rose—a well known or old reliable firm cannot risk putting out something new without first trying it in nearly all sections of the country. I have had the privilege of trying many new introductions before they were actually offered to the public and even when the reports were good, some were rejected as not suitable in all respects. Seldom do the nurseries get the new introductions until they are on the market one or two years. This means then that most of the new ones are sold directly by mail order. Generally the roses handled by dime stores, super-markets, etc., are the "old standards" mentioned. Occasionally a few of the recent introductions will appear in specialized markets. Some of the better local nurseries will often make arrangements to sell brand new introductions.

* * * *

During my photo expeditions and visits to the rose fields around Tyler, Texas, I observed two hybrid teas that never showed any sign of wilt during the heat of the day. They were the very excellent red rose CHRYSLER IMPERIAL and the two-tone McGREDY'S SUNSET. Also, the white floribunda called SUMMER SNOW withstood the terrific heat of Texas and Georgia.

* * * *

When you receive a rose catalog you seldom find more than 30 to 40 of the best known hybrid teas, plus from two to ten of the newer introductions. Among the reds will be such names as AMI QUINARD, BETTER TIMES, ETOILE DE HOLLANDE, POINSETTIA, RED RADIANCE,

Roses for Florida

ROUGE MALLERIN, TEXAS CENTENNIAL, GRENOBLE, ZULU QUEEN (which is a very dark blackish red).

Pinks include: BETTY, UPRICHARD, BRIAR-CLIFFE, EDITOR McFARLAND, PICTURE, PINK DAWN, PINK RADIANCE, THE DOCTOR.

Yellows include: ECLIPSE, GOLDEN CHARM, JOANNA HILL, LUXEMBOURG, MRS. P. S. DuPONT, SOEUR THERESE.

Whites include: K. A. VICTORIA, F. K. DRUS-CHKI, KONIGIN LUISE, WHITE BRAIRCLIFF.

Two-tone roses: CONDESA, DE SASTAGO, COUNTESS VANDAL, TALISMAN, McGREDYS SUNSET.

＊ ＊ ＊ ＊

Patented roses of recent years include the following: Among the reds are CHARLOTTE ARMSTRONG, CHRYSLER IMPERIAL, HAPPINESS, MIRANDY, NEW YORKER, NOCTURNE, RUBAIYAT, CORNADO, SUSPENSE, BINGO, AMERICANA. Among the whites are BLANCHE MALLERIN, REX ANDERSON, SLEIGH BELLS. Among the Pinks are HELEN TRAUBEL, ENCHANTMENT, SUZON LOTTHE, SYMPHONIE, TIFFANY, MY CHOICE, NOBILITY. Among the yellows are DIAMOND JUBILEE, FRED HOWARD, LOWELL THOMAS, PEACE, PUREGOLD, SUNLIGHT. Among the two tones with some yellow and other colors are DUET, FORTY-NINER, MOJAVE, SUSPENSE. This is only a partial list, there are many more to be found in the various catalogs.

GRANDIFLORA ROSES

Rosarians have come up with another type of rose classified as the GRANDIFLORA. They combine the best qualities and characteristics of both the hybrid teas and the floribundas which are their parents. In general they are tall, free-flowering plants which produce long stem cutting roses and also clusters of flowers. Flower size falls between those of the hybrid teas and the floribundas. The All American winner for 1955 was a pure pink rose called QUEEN ELIZABETH. This one has done well in Florida gardens. In 1956 came MONTEZUMA with long pointed orange-scarlet buds opening to salmon orange. Others followed such as ROUNDELAY, a dark red graniflora. STARFIRE, with shades of red and very luminous BUCCANEER, a brilliant non-fading yellow. CARROUSEL, a dark red with large bloom clusters and some single specimens. EBONY is one of the newest in dark velvety red. PINK PARFAIT, a 1961 grandiflora with delicate pink and creamy pastels. BEN HUR, another deep red with dark green shiny foliage.

CLIMBING ROSES

The so-called CLIMBING ROSES may be found in hybrid teas, polyanthas, and most all other kinds. Grafted on a special rootstock they live up to their name and really climb on trellis, lattice, buildings, fences, etc. One of the old reliables that does well in Florida is MARECHAL NIEL with its double deep yellow blooms that are very fragrant. Another old favorite is climbing MAMAN COCHET, or the white MAMAN COCHET. There is a climbing version of the famous PEACE ROSE available. Also the Talisman, Etoile de Hollande, and the true Sweetheart Rose CECILE BRUNER.

MINIATURE ROSES

There are some true miniature gems among the roses. Some of the blooms are the size of a quarter, and some as big as a fifty cent piece. In 1934 the late Robert Pyle of the rose firm Conard-Pyle Co. in West Grove, Pa., introduced the first patented minature rose which was called TOM THUMB. He brought many of the miniatures of John de Vink of Holland to this country and

Rosa Rouletti a delightful pink miniature rose.

started the demand for little roses. Today there is quite a long list of these delightful Fairy Roses available from rose firms and plant dealers. Nearly all of them are real hardy and suitable for outdoors Florida or for growing in pots or boxes on the patio or even in sunny areas of a Florida room. Even children like to make necklaces or

Roses for Florida

bracelets from these "Lilliputians" of the rose kingdom. Here is a partial list of some available Fairy roses: BO-PEEP (pink), BABY GOLD STAR (yellow), CENTENNIAL MISS (double rose-red), CINDERELLA (white), CUTIE (pink), FROSTY (white), JULIETTE (red), LEMON DROP (tiny yellow), LILAC TIME (lilac pink), MIDGET (red-rose), OAKINGTON RUBY (red), PATTY LOU (rose bi-color), PEGGY GRANT (shell pink), PIXIE (white), RED IMP (bright red).

Not all catalogs feature miniature roses. Write to the following firms:

Miniature Roses Dept. A.
4121 Prospect, (Catalog 25c)
Yorba Linda, Cal. 92686

Mini-Roses, Station A
Box 4255 K., Dallas, Tex. 75208

Thomasville Nurseries
Thomasville, Ga.

Winter Haven Nurseries, Inc.
1320 S. Lake Shipp Drive
Winter Haven, Fla. (Fla. Roses)

HOW TO PLANT ROSES

Here are some of the major steps recommended by rose experts for the planting of rose bushes: No. 1—Prepare a bucket or pail filled with thick muddy water. Unpack plants and soak the roots in muddy water for 6 to 8 hours. If not convenient to plant right away, then cover roots with soil, then cover tops with wet burlap or straw. No. 2—Dig beds to depth of 2 feet with hole large enough for roots. Ideal mixture to fill the planting hole is about 25% peat moss (or compost) and a handful of bonemeal or any special rose food. Soluble plant food can be used effectively, using one gallon to each planting hole. No. 3—Set the bush so that the graft (knob) will be at ground level. Pack the soil that is mixed with compost and plant food firmly around roots. When hole is half filled, pour in the bucket of water or mixed soluble plant food and fill with rest of soil. The top portion of hole needs a good portion of plant food, peat moss or compost. Space hybrid tea roses 16 to 18 inches apart, and Floribundas 18 to 24 inches. No. 4—For winter protection in case of cold spells (seldom needed in Florida) hill the soil 8 to 10 inches above ground level. Additional protection, in case of freeze, includes covering plants with straw, leaves or other material. No. 5—Mulch with leaves such as Java Plum or other trees, peat, straw, hulls, or well matured sawdust.

GENERAL ROSE CARE

The greatest enemy of the rose is the disease blackspot (Diplocarpon rosae) which causes the bushes to lose their leaves. When the disease attacks there is a gradual yellowing of the leaves. Many research programs have tried to find out how the fungus that is responsible for blackspot attack is related to the loss of leaves. So far, effective controls have come about, but there is the

Blackspot on rose leaves.

question—why do leaves drop off on some plants when only a portion of the leaf is affected, while in other instances leaves remain on the plant even after they are extensively infected by the fungus? Some lay the blame on nutritional deficiencies, others on dew and watering. Actually the answer is still a mystery and still in the future. Most hybrid teas, and a good many floribundas have to be dusted or sprayed in order to keep your rose bushes healthy. There are a number of good roses that seem almost immune to blackspot in certain areas, but will succumb in another part of the country or even the state. Old-fashioned tea roses seldom have much trouble, but now and then certain ones will have a light, but not disastrous attack. Many hybridizers have come up with roses that are free or almost free from blackspot, and there is a constant hunt for breeding stock with resistant qualities.

Roses for Florida

WATERING YOUR ROSES

Use a soaker to apply water to the bases. If you use a hose, then let it run slowly moving it now and then. If sprinklers are used, allow enough time for foliage to dry before sundown. It is claimed that water left on foliage after sundown is the cause of blackspot. Some growers recommend a foliage spray with minor elements or chelates once every 4 to 6 weeks. With a good balanced rose food this is seldom necessary. Just what effect chlorinated water has on roses is still much in debate. Personally, I prefer good well water or better still some good old rain water. Remember, roses need good drainage and do best in full sun.

DUSTING OR SPRAYING

There are scores of rose dusts and sprays on the market today, and the majority are effective if used as directed. It usually takes some pressure to apply rose dusts properly. There are a number of hand-cranked machines on the market that will throw an 8 foot stream of dust with only one or two cranks of the handle. This type is best where you have a number of rose bushes or fairly large beds. For just a few bushes, there are dusts available with a built-in device for dusting. Apply dusts when the morning dew is on the plants. Do not use dusts on blooming plants. For this purpose it is better to use rose spray instead. Most of the special sprays like the special dusts have enough controls for blackspot, mildew, insects and other pests. The most effective controls in recent years contain Captan or Fermate (Ferbam.) Massey Dust which consists of sulphur and lead arsenate is used by many rose growers. The Geo. W. Park Seed Co. of Greenwood, S. C. claims that the following LIME-SULPHUR formula is one of the old reliable controls for most diseases and pests of roses. It can be made at home.

Two pounds of fine powdered sulphur.

One pound of hydrated lime

One gallon of water.

Mix together and boil for one hour. Let the solution settle and bottle the clear solution for future use. When ready to spray—use one part clear solution to six parts water. In other words one quart solution to 6 quarts of water. You may add a few drops of powdered lime to give color to the foliage to designate where the spray has been used. Warning: this gives an odor when being mixed, so better prepare it outside.

ABOUT PRUNING

There is no set height to prune all roses. You may cut a bush two feet high down to 18 inches, but you wouldn't cut one four feet high down that low. One rule to follow, is not to take off more than ¼ the total height of the bush. Most rose growers recommend using a pruning paint on all cut stem ends. One made and sold in Florida is De-Ka-Go (Fasco Brand). It will even stick on fresh cuts. Treating of cuts helps in preventing disease, and also keeps the sawfly from boring into cut ends of tender growth. Dead limbs can be cut anytime, however the best time to prune in Florida is when there is an apparent dormant time about January or February. Canes that arise from the base of plants form the framework of the rose bush. Laterals are the branching stems from the canes. There are also some sub-laterals that form. Prune all laterals which are weak or diseased, especially those growing toward the center of the bush, and those that rub in the wind. Strong laterals growing in desirable directions are merely shortened to a good plump eye at a point which will make a well placed new branch or sublateral. After a rose has grown into the second season, and if you find the canes more or less crowded, then remove some of the older ones cleanly at the base with a pruning saw. The remaining healthy canes are then cut back one third. or enough to make a well-shaped bush.

GENERAL ROSE INFORMATION

Cut faded blooms back to a five-leaflet leaf. Make the cut about ¼ inch above a leaf joint (axil). If you use a mulch, be sure and add extra nitrogen now and then. Add an ounce or two of inorganic ammonium phospate during the growing season. This material is high in nitrogen, and even higher in phosphorous and both are in soluble form, and hence readily available when water or rain is applied. Best time to apply is when the plants are in heavy flower, which will be every 30 to 40 days.

It is possible to root certain roses by inserting cuttings in a slit Irish potato. You may apply Rootone or similar compounds to cutting.

Fragrant and Flowering Shrubs

THE WORD JASMINE suggests fragrance and the Old South. In fact some of the "Ol' Timers" called nearly all fragrant flowering shrubs or vines a Jasmine of some kind, and like most common classifications of plants, they're about 90% wrong. Even the very popular gardenia was once called the Cape Jasmine, and even though it has as much fragrance as any true jasmine, it is actually a member of the MADDER (*Rubiaceae*). Likewise with the so-called Day or Night Blooming Jasmines, they are quite fragrant but are actually CESTRUMS and belong to the *Solanaceae* family.

Even if a plant is not a true jasmine in a botanical sense, it may be just as fragrant or beautiful and just as useful in our gardens or landscapes. We will consider both the true jasmines and the so-called jasmines, and other flowering and fragrant shrubs suitable for Florida and Gulf Coast area.

WHAT ARE TRUE JASMINES?

The famous horticultural authority L. H. Bailey states that the true jasmines belong to the *Oleaceae* (Olive) family and placed in the genus JASMINUM. He also classifies the jasmines into three different leaf varieties, as follows: UNIFOLIA, which means the leaflets are only one, and as if they were truly simple leaves. Examples include Jas. gracile, pubescens. TRIFOLIATA which means the leaflets are three. Examples include Jas. nudiflorum, Jas. dichotomum, the famous Gold Coast Jasmine. PINNATIFOLIA which means more than three leaflets. Examples include the Poet's Jessamine or Jas. officinale, and Jas. humile.

Another horticultural authority the late Dr. Henry Nehrling states that there are as many STAR JASMINES as there are Johns in the Smith family, however the true STAR JASMINE is the one called Jasminum gracillimum of the unifoliata group and has simple ovate-lanceolate leaves about an inch to two inches long and a dark green color. The white flowers average an inch or more across. Excellent pot plant, or may be trained as vine.

Jasmine Pubescens is another good climbing type that has been frequently called a Star Jasmine. Its leaves (ovate and accuminate) will average from 1½ to 2 inches long. Stems are more or less downy. Jas. Pubescens bears dense clusters of white flowers an inch or more across, and is most profuse during the Autumn months. Be sure to allow space for it to ramble, and you may cut back any time of the year. Many people use the flowers and foliage for arrangements. In the cooler

Jasmine Pubescens

areas it may be nipped by frost during the Winter months, however they are very hardy and usually make a come-back in warm weather. *Jasminum gracillimum* has more pointed petals and finer stems than *Jas. pubscens*, but both do well in full or partial shade, and fairly well in full sun.

Another popular jasmine with many localized names is properly called SPANISH GRANDIFLORUM. It is perhaps best known as the ROYAL or SPANISH JASMINE or even the ITALIAN CATALONIAN Jasmine. This one bears pure white flowers from one to two inches across. There is a smaller-flowered version known as the POET'S JASMINE or *Jas. Officinale*. Both types have pinnate leaves (which means feather - formed) on slender branches and arranged in opposites (5 to 7 ovate leaflets to 2½ inches long with the terminal leaflet being much larger than the others.) Both the grandiflorum and the officinale will assume large proportions in time, but can easily be pruned into shape or size. They will stand as much as 10 to 12 degrees Fah., but they don't like wet feet. A very popular Jasmine that is often sold as a STAR JASMINE is properly called *Jasmine illicifolium*. This one has pointed glossy leaves in opposite pairs and bears loose clusters of white flowers with 8 to 11 pointed petals, and usually there is a trace of pink or purplish coloring on the underside. The buds are mixed with green and purple coloring. Individual flowers range from one inch to 1½ inces across, and

Fragrant and Flowering Shrubs

the flowering season is usually late Winter-Spring, however in some areas they seem to bloom most all year. This is a very willowy shrub, however it may be trained as a vine. Like all the jasmines, it can be easily started from cuttings.

The GRAND DUKE Jasmine is perhaps the closest rival in flower size and fragrance of the gardenia. Its flowers measure from 1½ to 2½ inches across and range from semi-double to a complete double, and they are intensely fragrant. Botanically it is called *Jasminum Sambac*, and is often referred to as one of the Arabian Jasmines. Another Arabian Jasmine that is smaller and bears single or semi-double flowers with more foliage is commonly called the MAID OF ORLEANS. This one is best suited as a trailing vine or to cover porches, slat houses or trellis, etc. The Grand Duke Jasmine is best suited as a shrub or may be used in same manner as gardenias, however they may need frequent trimming after the first year or two. Its foliage is much larger than the Maid of Orleans, but both belong to the unifoliate group. In warm areas such as Central and South Florida both types seem to be perpetual bloomers. Their flowers are white, but often take on a purplish tinge after a few days. Propagation is by cuttings.

As we stated the true STAR JASMINE is *Jas. gracille or gracillimum* (also listed as simplicifolium) and has white flowers with sharp pointed petals and branched or forked panicles. In recent years an improved Star Jasmine has appeared on the market, and is well suited as a pot plant. This one bears pinkish-white flowers that are sweet scented, and blooms most all year around in warm areas. It's botanical name is *Jasminum alisaefolium*.

No doubt there are many hundreds of white jasmines to be found the world over that haven't come to the limelight. Some are perhaps natives, and others are sports or they have been crossed. Not all true jasmines bear white flowers. There are many truly yellow Jasmines well suited for Forida and other warm areas.

Jasmine Gracille (Simplicifolium)

YELLOW FLOWERING JASMINE

Besides the all white jasmines and those tinged with pink, purple, etc., there are a number of excellent yellow flowering vines and shrubs that are classified as true jasmines. One that originally came from China, but is more or less considered a native in Florida and other warm areas, is commonly called the PRIMROSE JASMINE or *Jasminum primulinum*. The two-inch flowers (with a short corolla-tube and a leafy calyx that is longer than the tube) are primrose yellow with a darker yellow eye zone. Some bushes occasionally bear double flowers. In the warmer areas this twiggy, almost erect shrub will reach to ten feet in height. It is not considered a climber, but because of its drooping habit of growth, it is often called a vine, and has long pendulous green four-angled branchlets and small dark green foliage.

The PRIMROSE JASMINE is one of the finest plants for base plantings around houses and other buildings, or for mass plantings on the lawn. In Florida it has two blooming seasons, Spring and early Winter. Hardy in almost all areas of Florida. Also does well in South Georgia and Alabama, and similar areas. Although the Primrose jasmine is *Jas. primulinum* in botanical circles, some still classify it as *Jas. mesnyi*.

Another yellow flowering jasmine that is very hardy and considered to be a better bloomer than the Primrose, is called *Jasminum floridum*. The flowers and foliage are much smaller, however it is suitable for either specimen shrubs or for base or mass plantings. Both types belong to the trifolia or pinnatifolia group, and start easily from cuttings. Seeds are used, if obtainable. You may get the *Jas floridum* and *Jas. frutican* seeds from Harry E. Saier, Dimondale, Mich.

The ITALIAN YELLOW JASMINE which has several botanical names such as *Jas. humile, revolutum, reevesii or triumphans* is one of the hardiest of all yellow-flowering types. It seems to grow with little or no care as far north as Maryland. It flowers in late Summer and often as late as December in most Florida areas, is very erect and almost tree-like in growth, and often reaches to a height of 20 feet. The flowers are fragrant and are borne in clusters and average about half an inch across. There is some variation in the so called Italian Yellow Jasmines, hence the variety of botanical names. Never-the-less they are the most common in cultivation.

Fragrant and Flowering Shrubs

One of the lesser known yellow jasmines that loses its foliage in the Winter, but is covered with bright yellow blossoms in the Spring is called *Jasminum nudiflorum*. Not a climbing type, but often reaches to 15 feet in height, and bears flowers which are about an inch across. The branchlets are four-angled.

THE NON-JASMINE GROUP

As we stated before, there are many fragrant and flowering shrubs and vines that include the word Jasmine or Jessamine in their common name, but are not true Jasmines according to botanical classification. Take for instance the CAROLINA YELLOW JASMINE (or Jessamine) which is one of our finest native vines and very hardy in most Southern States. It actually belongs in the family known as LOGANIA which contains several plants used in extracting drugs and poisons like strychnine, etc. Its botanical name is *Gelsemium sempervirens*, and in spite of its poison or drug associations and relatives, it is a very beautiful yellow flowering vine for covering fences, trellis, stumps, farm buildings, and in the general landscape. Many are found growing on the native cabbage palm, and in open hammocks, abandoned fields, thickets and swamps. In the Spring it produces vivid bell-shaped fragrant yellow blossoms in abundance. Seed pods that follow contain several small winged seeds about an inch long. Foliage is dark green and consists of short-stalked leaves (simple) in pairs. Carolina Yellow Jasmine is also known as Yellow Jessamine, Evening Trumpet-Flower, and perhaps other local names. The leaves and the roots are poisonous to chickens, horses, sheep and cattle, so it is best to keep it out of their ranges. Propagation is by air layers, ground layering or constant mist cuttings.

Many people are disappointed when they find that the shrubs called Night or Day Blooming Jasmines are not jasmines in a botanical sense. However, they insist that the association of fragrance and the romantic memories, etc., is sufficient for them. Well you may have it that way if you choose, but for the purpose of correctness both the Day Blooming and the Night Blooming jasmines are classified as CESTRUMS. Night Blooming Cestrum is *Cestrum nocturnum* (meaning night) and Day Blooming Cestrum is *Cestrum diurnum* (meaning day). Both shrubs will reach to 10 or 12 feet in ideal soil. The flowers of the Night Blooming Cestrum are tubular and slightly greenish in color and of intense fragrance that sometimes becomes overpowering to some people. They average about ¾ of an inch long and are very slender. In the Central and Southern areas of Florida they often bloom at frequent intervals during the year. Following the blossoms many half inch white berries are found, and they are sometimes called the Poison Berry bush, because if consumed by humans in quantities they are very harmful. They are used in the making of certain medicines.

Cestrum diurnum or the Day Blooming type bears white flowers half an inch long and with reflexed lobes. Leaves are fairly shiny on top (oblong to ovate) and range from 2½ to 3½ inches long. The *Cestrum nocturnum* leaves are much longer, often reach to 8 inches in length.

The birds like the black berries of the Day Blooming Cestrum, so evidently they are not poisonous as the white berries of the Night variety. Because of the many seeds that form on both types, you will have many volunteer seedlings that may be transplanted to cans or containers if you want more plants for other locations. It is an easy matter to start either Cestrum from softwood cuttings. Should your Cestrums die-back because of cold spells, they will most likely come back as soon as the weather is warm. Instead of being in the true jasmine or jessamine family they belong to the NIGHTSHADE family (or *Solanaceae*) which includes edibles like tomatoes, eggplants, potatoes and others and also flowering plants like the Petunia, Schizanthus, and poisonous plants like jimson weed, daturas, tobacco and others.

ORANGE JESSAMINE (or Jasmine) whose real name is *Murraya paniculata* is another popular shrub of the non-jasmine group. It belongs in the RUE (*Rutacea*) family which includes the various citrus, and probably accounts for the name Orange Jessamine. The white flowers are about the size of the average orange blossom and likewise they are very fragrant. This shrub is ideal for hedges as well as specimen plants. They can be trimmed much in the same manner as boxwood and are often used as a substitute in North Central Florida. Not recommended in the North or Northwest areas, except in warm pockets. If not trimmed as a hedge or otherwise they will sometimes reach to 10 or 12 feet. The foliage is small and very shiny and bright green on top. The Orange Jessamine has been called CHALCAS for years and it was formerly listed as Chalcas paniculata (also listed in old catalogs as Chalcas exotica). It is sold even today by old-time nurserymen as CHALCAS. Another name that caused confusion for years was *Triphasia trifoliat*. This is actually the name of the Lime-Berry which is a handsome shrub with white fragrant flowers and bears red berries with an aromatic pulp and truly a citrus essence in flavor. No matter whether the Orange Jessamine is called Chalcas or Triphasia the right accepted name now is *Murraya paniculata*, but under any name it is useful shrub for lower Central and South Florida. Easy to start from cuttings.

Fragrant and Flowering Shrubs

The very name CONFEDERATE JASMINE connects it with the Deep South, but again this is another plant that is not a true jasmine. It is more or less an evergreen vine that originally came from

Confederate Jasmine

Confederate Jasmine — Trachelospermum Jasminoides.

Malaya. The foliage is leathery and glossy green (sometimes rather dark green) color. In the early Spring and even later, the five-petaled pinwheel-like blossoms are born in panicles of white fragrant clusters. The Confederate Jasmine really is called *Trachelospermum jasminoides* and belongs in the Dogbane or Apocynaceae family which includes other vines and shrubs with jasmine names.

Archways or elaborate trellis, etc., are often used to grace the entrance to many homes or gardens, and often the setting for a Spring wedding. Being a high climbing vine, it is useful to adorn most anything that will hold it. In Central and South Florida it is a favorite to drape mailboxes. Some people associate the fragrance to the odor of freshly grated nutmeg.

The Confederate Jasmine is propagated from layering, and airlayering may be used for large diameter woody parts near the ground. Some have luck with cuttings of mature wood.

* * * *

ERVATAMIA is the name of another shrub that has so many names, that it is no wonder confusion exists. For years this shrub that bears waxy white flowers that resemble gardenias was called *Tabernae-montana coronaria* by garden enthusiasts and plant specialists. Then the florists created a demand for the flowers for corsage use and they used the name FLEUR D'AMOUR. In Asiatic countries the name is listed as CEYLON JASMINE, WAX FLOWER, EAST INDIAN ROSEBAY, or BROADLEAF ROSEBAY, CASHMERE Flower, and many other local names. In Florida perhaps the most common name has been CRAPE (or CREPE) JASMINE, and the flowers do have a crepey nature, especially on the edges. After all this confusion the botanists decided the right name and classification should be ERVATAMIA.

Now about the shrubs with this name attached. *Ervatamia coronaria* produces many pure white (they fade to yellowish later) almost scentless waxy flowers with overlapping wavy edged petals. Flowers average about one and a half inches across. There is a double flowered form called flore pleno or in other words *Ervatamia coronaria, var. florepleno.*

Ervatamia grandiflora has been tagged the Broadleafed Rosebay. It resembles the coronaria, but has a more robust habit of growth and larger leaves. This one has semi-double pure white flowers with a yellow eye. The leaves sometimes reach to 10 inches in length and usually are darker than Ervatamia coronaria.

A milky juice exudes from cut branches of both the Ervatamias described, and if you plan on using the flowers for corsages or otherwise. it is advisable to burn the stem ends in a small flame. This will keep them from wilting.

Fragrant and Flowering Shrubs

Ervatamias are fine for base planting or for specimens in full sun or partial shade. In the extreme southern portions of Florida, it is better to plant in semi-shady locations. They prefer soil slightly on the acid side, but not as acid as for gardenias or azaleas. They will usually stand the cold spells of Central and South Florida, and should they be damaged by a freeze, they make a comeback in time. May be grown in large tubs or containers in the colder areas, and moved inside during the Winter. Many are grown this way

ERVATAMIA CORONARIA (Crepe Jasmine)
Formerly called Tabernae-montana.

as far north as the Carolinas. Give them a spraying of nutrient solution now and then (made from soluble plant food) and feed with any good garden fertilizer in Spring and Fall. Occasionally the Ervatamias will set a three-ribbed seed from one to three inches long and spread like a pair of horns. The pulp has been used for red dye in Asia. Start from cuttings of mature wood.

STEPHANOTIS which is called the Wax-Flower or Madagascar Jasmine is another of the very fragrant vine-like plants that does well in South Florida and parts of South Central areas. This woody vine bears pure white flowers that look almost artificial, and have an odor suggestive of white hyacinths. They are 5-lobed and waxy, with lobes turned back they look like tiny stars on slender 2 inch long tubes. Stephanotis floribunda is a favorite for bridal bouquets, and is long lasting and extremely fragrant. Sometimes used for making perfumes. Needs support and some shade in extreme South Florida. Subject to rootknot in dry soil, so it's a good idea to provide a good mulch and moist soil. May be started from air-layering, cuttings or seed. Member of Milkweed (*Asclepiadaceae*) family.

OTHER FRAGRANT FLOWERING PLANTS

LADY-OF-THE-NIGHT is the common name of a very fragrant flowering shrub properly called *Brunfelsia americana* and is a member of the Solanaceae family. Rather slender shrub that reaches 4 to 8 ft. in height, and bears quantities of fairly large white flowers on long slender tubes, and with a pungent delightful odor that permeates the atmosphere at night. Fine plant for the moonlight garden or for the patio. Glossy dark green foliage. Will grow in sun, but likes partial shade best. Prefers soil not too dry. Easily started from cuttings.

Besides the white-flowered *Brunfelsia americana*, there are a number of others that bear bluish, lavender, purple or bluish-white flowers that change with age. One is *Brunfelsia Hopeana* that bears violet-blue changeable flowers. Another is *Brunfelsia calycina* with dark purple flowers 2 inches across. Variations include *Brunfelsia eximia and Brun. floribunda* with rich violet flowers with small white eye. There are perhaps many more variations found among the plants sold and grown in Florida. Because of the beauty,

Brunfelsia Hopeana (violet blue, changeable flowers.)

the fragrance and the ease of growing, more Brunfelsias should be grown as garden and patio plants.

* * * *

The SWEET OLIVE or *Osmanthus fragrans* is one of the finest of ornamentals that bears an abundance of small white fragrant flowers, and grows in almost all areas of Florida to the Georgia and Alabama lines. Leaves are oval to oblong and about 4 inches long, entire edge fine toothed. This plant is sometimes grown in the greenhouse in colder climates. It is slow growing,

Fragrant and Flowering Shrubs

but in time will reach to 30 feet. Easy to transplant in late Fall or early Winter. Starts from seed or easily propagated from cuttings of half-ripened wood. Bears olive-shaped fruits of bluish-black color. Not edible. *Osmanthus americanus* is a native olive found in woods from Florida to Carolinas. This one grows to 45 feet in wild state.

* * * *

VIBURNUMS are among the most popular ornamental and fragrant shrubs for Florida and other southern states. However, certain ones are especially adapted for Florida. One of the most popular is *Viburnum odoratissimum* with large glossy green leaves. This extraordinary tree-like shrub should be grown in isolated spots or where it can have space enough to develop its lower branches without interference from other shrubs or trees. When this is done, it assumes a form of unrivaled beauty. The flowers appear in April and are borne in terminal clusters. They are milky-white and slightly fragrant. Considered a rapid grower, and for general landscape work or even hedges it will grow to an average of 6 to 10 feet in height. Fruit or berries are red at first but eventually turn black. Relished by the birds.

Viburnum suspensum is another good Viburnum for most areas of Florida. It is a low and spreading, more or less dwarf type that is well suited for home foundation use. By pruning now and then, it makes a very good hedge. Its foliage is large and deeply veined, but rather rough. A very free bloomer with small cream colored flowers borne in clusters during Spring and Summer.

Viburnum japonicum (*macrophyllum*) is more upright in growth than *odoratissimum* and well suited for Central and Northern Florida. Seldom exceeds six feet. Excellent evergreen. Bears fragrant flowers in short-stalked cymes to 4 inches across. Fruit red.

Viburum tinus (*Laurestinus*) is one of the finer Viburnums, but not too well known in Florida. This evergreen reaches to 10 feet and bears white to pinkish flowers in 3 inch cymes. Foliage to 3 inch long and dark green above.

Viburnums belong in the same family as the honeysuckle (*Caprifoliacea*) and there are perhaps a hundred or more fine broadleaf evergreens in the list suitable for most Florida areas. Some of the lesser known Viburnums in Florida can be started from seed. (See Saier and other catalogs.) Easily propagated from cuttings otherwise.

* * * *

When we speak of fragrant plants or vines, it is usually taken for granted that we mean sweet fragrance. Well, there is a vine that produces some of the most beautiful lavender Gloxinia-like flowers at intervals during the year, yet it is called the GARLIC VINE. The leaves when crushed smell exactly like garlic. The true name of the vine has

another association, *Cydista aequinoctalis* (equinox) which means that it blooms heavy during the equinox or the season when the days and nights are of equal duration. This is an ideal vine for lower Central and South Florida and easily started from cuttings of mature wood. Very choice dark green foliage.

* * * *

The RANGOON CREEPER Vine (*Quisqualis indica*) is a very unusual vine that bears flowers that change from white to pink and finally to maroon color. At first this plant seems to be a shrub, then after a year or more, a runner will start at the base of the plant and from then on it becomes a rambling vine with stout but not vicious thorn-like projections all along the entire length. This sudden departure from shrub to vine is perhaps why the name Quisqualis which according to a Dutch story means "what goes on here." The flowers that remain for a long period of time start in the latter part of May and sometimes last until the latter part of June. They have 5 petals each and are very fragrant at night or early morning. Their fragrance is quite different from other fragrant plants we have described, sort of trace of vanilla may be detected. After blooming a curious nut or seed forms, which has five ridges and is about an inch or more long. These seeds or nuts are deep brown in color and appear in rosette fashion. The kernel inside is edible, and very pleasant. One warning, if you eat one too many you may get the hiccoughs. Many seedlings come up under the vine, and these may be transplanted or put in cans. It takes two years from seed to blooming plants, if grown in good moist soil. In addition to this it likes a good mulch. The leaves of the Rangoon Creeper are pointed and deeply veined and a little on the rough side. The vine is bare during the Winter months. Be sure and provide support for this rather heavy vine. Suitable for Pinellas County southward, or from Vero Beach southward on East Coast.

FRANGIPANI or Plumeria of the Dogbane family is another very unusual plant with fragrant flowers. This is the flower used in sacred or temple worship in India and often called the Temple-Flower. The bare shrub or tree is stick-like or some say like cigars and very grotesque in form, but as soon as real long leaves appear it takes a beautiful symmetrical form. Waxy tubular flowers up to 3 inches across are borne as late as November and have a delightful fragrance. Many colors and combinations are available. Pure white or creamy yellow, pink, rose, and rainbow mixtures may be had. A milky juice exudes from foliage, stems, flowers, and bruised parts of plant. Frangipani starts easily from the stick-like cuttings (even to a foot in length). Just stick one end in medium soil. Suitable for lower Central and South Florida areas.

Gardenias

IN FLORIDA and elsewhere in this country, the GARDENIA probably holds first place among the fragrant flowers. Grown on a large scale commercially, and nearly every home with yard or garden space has one or more gardenia bushes. Although we think of the gardenia as one particular white flower used for corsages and for fragrance, etc., there are hundreds of hybrid gardenias today that differ in size of flower, size of shrub, flower formation and foliage. Each of these hybrids have a name, and some have become standards in the nursery or florist trade. Before we get into part of the subject, let's go back to the Colonial days and to the beginning of the change from Cape Jasmine to that of Gardenia.

The genus GARDENIA was named in honor of a prominent Charleston, S. C. physician named Dr. Alexander Garden, responsible for much of its initial success as a florist and house plant. Gardenias are in the Rue (*Rubiacae*) or Madder family which includes Coffee, Ixora, Pentas and other well known Florida plants. Botanically the full name is *Gardenia jasminoides*. Old timers and many others still insist in calling any Gardenia a CAPE JASMINE or Jessamine. During the course of history of many plants such as the gardenia there often appears what is known as a mutation or sport, which means a sudden departure from the original, or they may be a bud sport, or a cross pollination that produces a superior plant or flower. No doubt this happened to the original gardenia for today we have many that either came by this route or by planned breeding and pollination.

The first of the newer named varieties to ap-

Gardenia Veitchii

pear on the American market actually came from the English firm of James Veitch and Sons, and it was named VEITCHII gardenia. Even today it is probably the most popular of all gardenias, but its waxy flowers are small in comparison to some of the other well known varieties. Gardenia Veitchii looks like a dwarf shrub when grown alongside the vigorous BELMONT which bears flowers four to five inches across, or the HADLEY which bears large flat blossoms in the Spring. The Hadley foliage is a much darker green that that of other gardenias. It is exceptionally good for commercial production.

The MIAMI-SUPREME Gardenia, which is a sport of the VEITCHII produces large flowers from four to six inches across and which are more resistant to bruising than most others, is a very popular one for shipping. The flowers are camellia-like with a central whorl and with 25 or more petals that open slowly.

For open air planting in Florida, the gardenia called MYSTERY is very popular. It produces heavily in April and May, is a quick opening type but not especially suited for shipping trade.

The gardenia that came from Honolulu under the name of GRANDIFLORA is a superior type with blossoms that measure about four inches across and with the very desirable central whorl. It averages about 36 petals per flower.

A gardenia that produces flowers about the size of a quarter is called *Gardenia RADICANS*. This miniature type seldom exceeds 18 to 20 inches in height for the bush, but does produce an abundance of fragrant blossoms. The foliage

The Belmont Gardenia — one of the large flowered hybrids.

is also small, with narrow leaves from half an inch to one and a half inches long.

Other popular named varieties of Gardenias that are available in Florida include the following: GLAZERII, CAMEO, McCLELLAN, JOAN DAISY HILL and many more that deserve recognition.

The original gardenias grew in swampy or low mucky areas that were very much on the acid side. They are therefore naturally acid-loving and belong in the group known as extreme acid-loving plants, which include Camellias, Azaleas, Hydrangeas, Red Bud, Magnolia, and others. When grown in their natural habitat the gardenias never required any special understock or grafting. As most of the plants are grown in the average garden, it is best to buy plants that have been grafted on what is known as *Gardenia thunbergia* stock which is resistant to nematodes or rootknot. Although most of the *Gardenia thunbergia* grown today are used to understock all the various *Gardenia jasminoides* mentioned (and others), it is a wonderful fragrant flowering shrub in its own right. It produces large white flowers with a long tube, but not suitable for cutting or other uses of the regular gardenia. If allowed to grow for many years, it will reach a small tree's proportion.

GRAFTING PROCEDURE

Gardenia thunbergia seedlings are grown in cans or pots until they reach pencil size, then they are grafted by the side-graft, splice, or whip-graft method. Seedlings that are from 10 to 12 inches high are used. A deep sloping cut about 6 or 8 inches above the pot is made, then a prepared terminal scion from a regular gardenia is sharpened to a long sloping wedge shape to fit into the slot. This scion should be about three inches long and with two to four leaves remaining. When the cambiums are carefully aligned, bind with rubber budding strips (which may be purchased at your garden store). To exclude the air and water, the whole is waxed with a prepared grafting wax.

It is a good idea to place the grafted plants in a case with a glass top about 10 to 12 days. Then gradually let in a little air each day for the 10 or 12 days, then remove glass or top completely. When the graft scion (regular gardenia) has grown a few inches, you remove the top of the Gardenia thunbergia by cutting just above the graft union. The rubber budding strips will soon begin to disintegrate and fall away. Note: If you start your root stocks of thunbergia, it will take from four to six months to reach grafting size. Some nurseries sell rootstocks already for grafting.

GROWING AND FEEDING GARDENIAS

Because of their acid-loving nature, it is best to supply gardenias with plenty of organic matter, peat, humus, leaf-mold, sawdust, etc., in the plant-ing hole or the container. Composted materials are available at most garden stores, or you may use your own. Acidifying elements like aluminum sulphate, alum, and even vinegar are used by many growers. Special gardenia (or azalea and camellia specials) formula are sold with the necessary acidifying elements added. (See April Garden Calendar). If you plant gardenias in the open ground, then a good mulch should be used. This can be oak leaves, Java Plum leaves, matured sawdust, peat, pine straw, water hyacinths, and hulls or pods.

Besides feeding with special gardenia fertilizer formulas, it is helpful to use a foliage spray such as Minorel or Sesquestrene once every 6 to 8 weeks. Do not spray when in bloom or when buds are ready to open. Minorel elements supplied in this way help give that healthy green appearance to the leaves.

In the real warm areas of Florida, it is best to plant gardenias where they can get some filtered shade during the heat of the day. Certain varieties will take the heat better than others. Too much shade invites sooty mold caused by whiteflies.

PESTS AND DISEASE

Planting gardenias that haven't been grafted on thunbergia understock in the general run of soils will usually bring on most anything from sickly yellow plants to heavy infestation of nematodes that cause root knot and eventual dying of the plant. Of course there are some soil fumigants on the market that often help, but are not as dependable as an immune understock.

Yellowing of leaves is known as chlorosis, or a deficiency of certain mineral elements. The nutrient spray mentioned will usually take care of this situation. Yellowing also may be caused by neutral or alkaline soils, or possibly from too much water. A pinch of Iron Sulphate to each plant in pots or soil will often stop the yellowing.

SOOTY MOLD is one of the worst enemies of the gardenia. It is a black fungus growth found on the upper side of the leaves. Insects such as the whitefly, aphids, and mealybugs discharge a honeydew that nurtures the sooty mold and causes the plants to have a dirty appearance.

For control of sooty mold and yellowing, use an oil spray such as VOLCK OIL SPRAY or LIN-OIL and combine with improved ISOTOX GARDEN SPRAY M, or with BLACK LEAF 40. Soapy water is helpful to remove sooty mold when it first starts. The pickle-vinegar method (April Garden Calendar section) is also helpful.

Greenhouse gardenias are sometimes attacked by what is known as Greenhouse Orthezia which is an insect related to the scale insects and mealybugs. Female is dark green and has marginal fringe and long fluted egg sac extended from the back of the body. Isotox Garden Spray M and oil will control this pest.

Bulbs and Tuberous-Rooted Plants

TO MANY PEOPLE call the various bulbous or tuberous plants a bulb, when actually it may be a corm, tuber, rhizome or tuberous root. So that you will know the difference, and make better use of the chart that follows, we will define or describe the various classifications that make up the thousands of plants of the bulbous or tuberous nature. A very large number belong to the Amaryllid family, lesser numbers are in the Lily or Lilium family, and also the Aroid (*Araceae*) family. There are many hundreds of plants that have the name Lily attached to their common name, but are not in the true lily family.

EASTER LILY (Lilium Longiflorum)

In the chart you will find the true botanical name and classification, and also the common name, if there is one in common usage.

* * * *

The Easter Lily and the Onion both come from bulbs, but there is quite some difference in appearance, but very little difference in general. Lily bulbs are actually modified stems surrounded at the base with fleshy scales (which are modified leaves) folded around the central bud. This type of bulb is referred to as the scaly BULB. The bulb of the Onion has a tight-fitting skin or tunic, and this type is called the "tunicated bulb". Tulip bulbs are also of the tunicated type. In other words in a true bulb there is an entire blooming plant with stems, leaves and flowers all telescoped into a convenient package, and which will keep the plants at rest in adverse climates.

In some species of lilies small BULBLETS are produced in the axils of the leaves above the ground. After ripening, they should be planted immediately. Most of the stem-rooting lilies produce BULBELS on the underground stem. In other words, the small bulbs produced between the scales and inside the bulb are called BULBELS, and those produced in the axils of leaves are called BULBLETS. The Tiger Lily produces new bulbs in three places: (1) Bulblets in the axils of the leaves (2) Above the old bulbs underground (3) Natural offsets at base. Oxalis, Tuberose and Narcissus produce many Bulbels. The Multiplier or Potato Onion produces many Bulblets.

* * * *

CORMS differ from bulbs in that a greater part is more or less solid and is not stem, but scales which are thickened bases of leaves. The stem is merely a flattened plate from which root and bulb scales arise.

Corms are covered with shells or scales which are known as husks or tunics. The scales are likewise the bases of leaves, but not thickened as in the bulbs. Nearly all corms are produced below the soil. One of the best known producers of corms is the GLADIOLUS. Every gladiolus stem that shows vigorous growth has a corm at its base. Nearly every corm has several buds and each one that grows will produce a new corm on top of the old one in the soil. Reports indicate that as many as seven blooming-size corms will form on a single plant in a season. It usually takes one to four years (depending on variety) for a seedling to produce a corm of blooming size. One thing to keep in mind, if you want your glads to produce more corms, be sure and not cut the bloom spikes too low. Leave enough foliage to properly mature the corm. The vigor and thickness of the corm depends on following this rule. Other plants that produce corms include Monbretia, Watsonia, Ixia, Crocus, Cyclamen, Colchicum, Morae, Sparaxis and Tigridia.

* * * *

CORMELS are small corms that are found between the old and new corms, when the base of the Gladiolus stems begin to thicken. Cormels differ from the seedling (from seed) glad of the same size in that they have a hard shell instead of the husk or dried base of the previous season's leaves. Because they are hard, it is sometimes necessary to soak them in order to soften the hard shells.

Bulbs and Tuberous-Rooted Plants

RHIZOMES are underground stems. They are creeping stems (above or below the soil) with buds or eyes, also with scales representing leaves. Sometimes a Rhizome is simply referred to as a ROOT-STOCK, and most of them can be divided for propagation. Not all rhizomes are thick or fleshy for some are as fine as wire. Bermuda grass is an example of a fine rhizome. Bamboos produce rhizomes, likewise Cannas, Callas, Aspidistra, Maranta, Lily of the Valley, and many others.

There are many ferns and water-lilies that produce rhizomes. Rhizomes should be planted horizontally, however if you know which is the upper end they can be planted vertically. When starting new plants, select a piece that bears one or two eyes.

The following garden plants produce Rhizomes: Achimenes, Bloodroot, Iris, Plumbago, Wildginger, Heleborous, Funkia or Hosta, Acanthus, Monstera, Primula Sieboldi.

* * * *

TUBERS are the thickened portion of stems on certain plants and are usually produced beneath soil. They have buds or eyes from which growth will start. Irish potatoes are an example of the tuber, also other edibles like the Taro or Dasheen, and the Artichoke. The popular Climbing Lilies or Gloriosa Lilies are producers of tubers shaped like an L or a V. This one can be broken in two pieces at the natural junction and each will become a new plant. Small tubers (with rounding protruding body) are sometimes classified as TUBERCLES. A good example is the ACHIMENE which grows from tiny tubercles that form on the roots, and which will remain dormant through the winter months after the plant has died down in late fall.

TUBEROUS ROOTS have no buds or eyes. Their eyes are actually at the base of the old flowering stem. Examples of the tuberous-root plants include the Dahlia, Tuberous Begonia, Boussinggaultia or better known as the Madeira Vine, also the Caladium, and *Hemerocallis dumortieri*.

* * * *

Those sometimes unexpected shoots from the base of such plants as the Banana, Heliconias, Pandanus, Pineapples, Billbergias, Aechmeas, Agaves (Century Plants) are called SUCKERS. All suckers may be pulled or broken from the parent plant, to start new plants. Certain plants like the Walking Iris or Marica, Aloes, Aechmeas, Billbergias, Pineapples, Escheveria, Sempervivums, and others produce small plantlets which if allowed to reach the soil or other mediums will root easily and form new plants. These are called OFFSETS.

Philippine Lily — Summer Easter Lily.

CONSIDER THE LILIES

Although the State of Florida is not considered a lily area, it does have a large commercial acreage in Easter Lilies in the vicinity of Sebring and Lake Placid and some scattered plantings. There are perhaps less than a dozen true lilies that grow in the state, and most of these are grown in the northern sections. However in recent years many new lilies have been tried in Central and South Florida, and some success has been reported. From my own tests of the Philippine Lily (*Lilium formosanum*) I believe that it could be raised on a large scale on the Gulf Coast or through the Central areas. This lily equals the Easter Lily in beauty and could be called one except for one reason, they bloom in the late Summer months.

The true Easter Lilies are known as *Lilium longiflorum*, and there is a strain or variety that is known as *Lilium longiflorum Floridii* that is best suited for most areas of Florida. They produce blooms within 110 to 130 days. Most growers stagger the plantings so there is more assurance of getting blooms in time for the Easter trade. If you want yours to bloom for Easter, be sure and buy bulbs of from 4 to 6 inches in circumference. The larger the better. If planted later, you can sometimes force blooms by feeding with soluble plant foods once a week for three months, and then once every two weeks. Be sure and include some humus in your planting containers. Many other varieties or strains of Easter Lilies are offered in seed or bulb catalogs under such names as Bermuda Easter Lily, Creole Lily (from Louisiana), Croft Lily, and a good many Japanese importations.

The following true lilies also grow in Florida under some conditions: GOLD-BANDED LILY (*Lily Auratum*), MADONNA LILY, (*Lily candidum*), REGAL Lily (*Lilium regale*), RUBRUM Lily (*Lilium rubrum*), TIGER Lily (*Lilium tigrinum*).

Bulbs and Tuberous-Rooted Plants

PLANTS WITH LILY NAMES

There are many beautiful plants that are lily-like in appearance to many people, and some of them even have the name lily included in their common name, but are not included in the true lily family. Take for instance the **Milk and Wine Lilies, The Spider Lilies, Daylilies, Rain Lilies** and many more. A large majority of the popular ones in Florida belong to the Amaryllid family which includes the very popular Dutch and American strains of hybrid Amaryllis offered in a wide variety of color and patterns and really set off a garden or landscape. September and October are the ideal months for planting Amaryllis. Blooming season starts in January (if warm weather) on through April and sometimes into May and June. They usually precede and overlap the Daylilies.

CRINUMS BEST SUBSTITUTE FOR LILIES

MILK AND WINE Lilies or CRINUMS are associated with the South as much as Camellias and Jasmines. The lily-like blooms are white and red striped in the so called **Milk and Wine** group. The following are considered Milk and Wine Crinums (or lilies) ; *Cri. Kenthianum, Cri. Erubescens, Cri. Campanulatum, Cri Zeylanicum.*

Among the other Specie Crinums that are excellent for gardens, walks, near pools, and which do well in most all areas of Florida are the following: *Crinum Asiaticum* which is called the giant white "Spider Lily", *Crinum Amabile* which produces rose-purple and white highly perfumed blossoms and giant leek-like bulbs; *Crinum bulbispermum* (also Capense or longiflorum) one of the first to bloom with blue-green foliage and pink and white flowers. Hardy in most Southern States; *Crinum Moorei* a beauty but tender in colder areas; *Crinum Scabrum* a dwarf scarlet type with short stems; *Crinum Giganteum* as the names suggest is large, and it produces large white tulip-like flowers and likes shady places. CHRISTOPHER LILY which is another favorite in Florida is a *Cri. Giganteum* hybrid and preferred by many.

CRINUM "Ellen Bosanquet"

CRINUM HYBRIDS include some extraordinary blossoms, and one of the most famous is the one called CECIL HOUDYSHEL Crinum which is a free-blooming variety bearing large umbels of clear pink trumpet-shaped blooms on tall stems. This one is excellent for mixing in with Daylilies. One of the most showy of the hybrids is called ELLEN BOSANQUET which bears large wine colored blooms. LOUIS BOSANQUET produces light pink and white blooms and is an early blooming variety. A pure white Crinum that is choice and very outstanding is one known as *CRINUM POWELLI var. Album* (meaning white). Glossy green leaves up to 20 inches high with 3 to 7 bloom scapes bearing umbels of white lily-like flowers. Blooms for Easter in some areas. Will grow as far north as Carolina and Tennessee.

Pink — Louis Bosanquet Crinum

Bulbs and Tuberous-Rooted Plants

Pure White Crinum Powelli

The list of Crinums, hybrids and species keeps increasing, and they should be considered for Florida gardens of every type. Not requiring much, if any attention they reward you with beautiful flowers, foliage and perfume. Some produce large bulbs, others medium to small, and a good many set seed that are like a small bulb and may be used to start more plants.

One of the finest plants to grow under large oaks or other trees, or in shady or semi-shady places is the AMAZON Lily (also called EUCHARIST LILY). They like fairly moist soil, however most of them are grown in tubs or large containers, and thrive better when their roots are more or less constricted. They may be divided in the Fall. The flowers of the Amazon Lily are pure white and resemble those of the Narcissus, and are very fragrant. They are produced in clusters from three to six on stout stalks about 18 inches in height. Blooms in February or March. The Amazon Lily (*Eucharis Amazonica*) may be grown in pots for patio or porches. Use 5 or 6 bulbs for a 10 inch pot. Use a good compost or potting soil.

There are several plants commonly called SPIDER LILIES, however the true Spider Lily is known as *HYMENOCALLIS Caribea*. It grows in large clumps and flowers in dense masses in February and March. Flowers are pure white and fragrant. The foliage resembles that of the Amazon Lily slightly. Spider Lilies are useful in bouquets, or in making wreaths or crosses. At night the perfume is really intense and sometimes overpowering.

MILK AND WINE LILY A favorite Crinum since Civil War days.

SPIDER LILY (Hymenocallis Caribea)

48

Bulbs and Tuberous-Rooted Plants

The JACOBEAN Lily or SPREKELIA produces a very unusual flower of a very dark red or brilliant crimson, and which resembles certain orchids. They are considered hard to raise in Florida, but I have found that they have to be moved from year to year, that is the bulbs are allowed to rest for a period and planted in a new place. Plant bulbs in the Fall and in fairly alkaline soil. Sprekelia blooms make ideal corsage material, or are nice for arrangements.

* * * *

Among the large variety of Amaryllids there are a number of very beautiful miniatures such as the RAIN Lilies, ZEPHYR, FAIRY Lilies, or

AFRICAN BLOOD LILY (Haemanthus multiflorus.)
Beautiful foliage follows flowering head.

HABRANTHUS — RAIN LILIES

PRAIRIE Lilies. They are called Rain Lilies because they have a habit of blooming profusely after a good rain. Botanically they are known as *Zephyranthes*. Colors include pink, rose and shades of yellow. The larger flowered Rain Lilies are called HABRANTHUS. Texas Rain Lilies are known as COOPERIA. All of the Rain Lilies produce many paper thin seeds that may be used for starting more plants, however they mutiply fairly fast without using seeds. Zephyranthes of several kinds may be used in pots or for hanging baskets.

One of the most spectacular blooms is that found on the AFRICAN BLOOD Lily or *Haemanthus multiflorus*. The rounded head (umbels) of bright red flowers range in size from a grapefruit to large honey dew melon. This depends on the age or size of the bulbs planted. Each head is made of hundreds of small flowers each having a stigma and pollen-bearing stamens. You can assist in obtaining pollination by simply running the palm of your hand back and forth a few times over the entire flower-head. Later a number of reddish berry-like seeds will form, and when they are mature (birds like them) they can be planted. It will take three or four years to obtain a small blooming plant from seed or even from small bulbs that form around the mother bulb. Even after the bloom dies the Blood Lily makes an excellent foli-

age plant for a long time. They eventually die back with the cold weather. If used as a house or patio plant they may last up into the Winter months. After the foliage dies, you may leave the bulb in the ground or container and it will come back again in the Spring. If you prefer, it can be lifted and stored until late February, then planted again. Store in vermiculite or perlite. New bulbs will form each year, and you may leave them attached for a year or more if you like, and then separate, however they will most likely put out their own foliage even the first year. Although it takes from three to four years for the new bulbs to reach blooming size, some come into bloom at two years of age. A mature bulb is about the size of an Amaryllis bulb. Medium-size blooming bulbs average from 1½ to 2 inches. Blooming season is from April through July and occasionally later. *Haemanthus Multiflorus* is the best African Blood Lily for Florida, however now and then you will find *Haemanthus Katherine* in a greenhouse or collection. This one is best suited to California.

GLORIOSA Lilies are another spectacular blooming plant for Florida gardens, or for the patio or house plant usage. Sometimes they are commonly called the Climbing Lily, for they are vine-like in their habit of growth and must have something provided for support. The two most popular Gloriosa lilies are *Gloriosa Rothschildiana* and *Gloriosa Superba*, however there are many more hybrids and species from Africa, and India.

Gloriosa Rothchildiana produces showy crimson-scarlet and gold flowers with recurved segments. The whole flower gradually deepens in color as it matures. The V or L shaped plump tubers (which are brown at maturity) must be handled carefully to protect the bud-eyes on the tips. When ready to plant the tubers can be parted at an angle. Plant in the Spring or they may be handled like Gladiolus, that is, they can be planted at intervals of two or three weeks apart in order to obtain blooms every month of the year in most areas of Florida. Commercial growers dig and

Bulbs and Tuberous-Rooted Plants

plant the tubers at regular intervals to keep almost a continuous bloom. Many Gloriosas are grown in pots and greenhouses in colder climates.

The *Gloriosa Superba* is second in popularity and is more vine-like than *Rothchildiana*. They will grow all over a slat house or up in shrubs and trees. Some term the Superba a yellow variety, however it does deepen to a tawny red as it matures. It seems to follow the Rothchildiana in

CRINUM CECIL HOUDYSHEL

blooming, however the two may bloom at the same time. There is a bit of flexibility in these two Gloriosas, and they perform well most of the late Spring and Summer months. All the Gloriosa have curling tendrils at the tips of the leaves by which they attach themselves to strings, wire, or other supports. They set seed easily and form fairly large pods full of bright red seeds that may be planted later. They need a ripening period, and this may take from 10 to 12 months.

When planting the tubers of either variety, it is best not to use compost or manures, as this may cause scab or bulb rot. Use fertile soil that is well drained and a little commercial fertilizer or sol-

AMARYLLIS — Hybrid Type

uble plant food. Tubers may be stored in vermiculite or peat in a cool dry place.

Another Gloriosa that is gaining is one known as *Gloriosa Planti*. Smaller but similarly shaped to *Rothchildiana*, with broad petals only slightly waved or crisped. Coloring of flowers is yellow and orange. Like the others they deepen in color as they mature. There are many more Gloriosa lilies obtainable from plant specialists, but the first two mentioned serves the general public very well. All make excellent cut flowers or arrangement material. Many of the florists sell them for corsage use, much in the same manner as orchids.

It would take books to cover all the plants with the name Lily attached; we have covered some of the popular ones for Florida Gardens.

Daylilies

HEM-FEVER IS SWEEPING the country, and is prevalent in Florida. It is very contagious and may persist for years, once you become a victim. Hem-fever is really the yen to grow the plants commonly called the Daylily. Actually the daylily is not a true lily, and instead of deriving its food from bulbs, it comes from thick roots. They belong to the Amaryllid family, the generic name being *Hemerocallis*.

One writer describes the transformation of the old daylily to the aristocratic *hemerocallis* as another American success story. Once they were called common roadside lilies, tawny lilies, or lemon lilies, but now their wardrobe is so extensive that no one knows just how many thousands are grown in every state of this country and elsewhere. The Hemerocallis now ranks next to the Rose in the number of societies, and general popularity. There is a National Hemerocallis Society and many Regional branches. A monthly Journal is published and also a Yearbook.

Just why is the Daylily or Hemerocallis so popular: One might answer this by saying it is the easiest of all plants to grow, and one of the most rewarding for colorful flowers, and its freedom from insects and pests. On top of all this, they seem to thrive in prolonged periods of dryness, or where there is much rainfall. They don't mind the hot or the cold spells. In other words— even with maximum neglect they seem to thrive and even bear, however like all other plants, they do much better when some attention is given along with a general feeding and watering program. In Florida they thrive in almost any soil from mucky to dry sandy types. Certain varieties will not take swamp conditions, and certain ones don't particularly like sandy soil. Their dislike comes in time, so that you may move them to suitable soils and locations. The ideal soil is a medium loam with good drainage. If planted in good rich soil they need very little plant food. Two or three applications of soluble plant food during the year are usually sufficient. Foliage sprays of minor elements do help give a good green color to foliage. and brighter colors to the flowers.

Some growers recommend several light applications of a complete fertilizer such as 5-10-5 or 6-10-4 in the Spring or early Summer. Just be careful you don't get too much nitrogen in feedings, for this produces more foliage and less flowers.

Most daylilies will grow in full sun or the shade, however certain ones fade easily if they get too much sun during the day, and others don't flower heavily if grown in the sun. Plant enough varieties to provide blooms from one or the other, until you find the best ones to grow in any loca-

Daylilies

Daylily — Purple Wings.

Daylily — Hope

Daylily — Aunt Cliff
Aunt Cliff shows three-toned banded throat patterns. Produces tall scapes.

tion. Some catalogs specify if a variety is suitable for sun or shade.

The reason these popular plants are called Daylilies is that a flower opens every day of the week in regular order in each scape or stem. By planting many of one color, or several colors and mixtures, you can obtain some striking mass effects. By proper selection of varieties, you can also have an extended season of bloom. In Florida the first ones bloom in March (certain areas) or April, and occasionally some will bloom before March if the weather has been warm for long periods. The height of the season is from late April thru May. Some varieties bloom later and there are enough of them to extend the season through September. I had some still blooming in December when the weather was warm.

* * * *

During the first season, single plants should produce from one to three bloom stems. If left undisturbed they will multiply into good sized clumps within three to five years. You may divide them anytime after the first three years. Specialists recommend leaving clumps for four to five years before dividing. Best time to divide and transplant in Florida is September and October, however it is possible to do this almost any time of the year. As most plants are sold during the height of the blooming season, it often becomes necessary to divide at that time.

Daylily — Pods and Seeds.

Some Daylilies produce proliferations along broom-stalk. After flowering has ceased and all seed capsules are mature, cut above and below each proliferation and plant in same mixture recommended for seeds. They root easily and may be planted out later just as an established plant. Usually, they bear flowers the next season and are like the parent plant.

Applying pollen to daylily.

Daylilies

A good mulch is not a necessity, but it does help keep down weeds and conserve moisture and plant foods. Wood shavings, sawdust, leaves, spaghnum moss, are some of the items suitable for a mulch. If you use sawdust or shavings, apply some Milorganite to the soil first. This supplies enough extra organic nitrogen that will be needed.

ABOUT VARIETIES

There are perhaps some eight to 10,000 named varieties of Daylilies in gardens, catalogs, etc., in this country. More new ones are added each year. Originally, most of the colors were shades of yellow, orange, and red, but now you can get almost all colors except a true blue, solid green (there are some lime colored ones) and white. The goal of every hybridizer is a pure white Daylily. When this is accomplished, then the race starts all over again.

Some daylilies are all one color, or perhaps two almost identical colors, others have two or more mixtures in petals, sepals, throat. Some have what are known as eye-zone colors, throat-zone, and many other variations. Then there is wide variance in size and shape of blooms, starting with midget flowers on up to some 8 to 10 inches across. There are some with twisted petals, some with an orchid appearance, some with crepey edges, and a few other noticeable variations. Some flowers have a velvety or satin sheen, others are matte or dull appearing. Study a few catalogs of Daylily growers and specialists and you will discover many of these variations in the blooms illustrated. You will also notice many blooms have prominent or light center veins called "mid-rib" veins.

Some Daylilies are considered low-growers, with short stems or scapes, others are classified as medium, or tall growers. There are some real small types called dwarfs or midgets.

There are one or two double daylilies available, and they are mostly a deep orange or vermillion color. The foliage is broad on the double varieties. In Florida they start to bloom about May and last a little longer than the general run.

CREATING YOUR OWN HYBRIDS

It is easy to achieve your own daylily hybrids. This is the last stage of the Hem-Fever mentioned, and seldom do you recover. First dose is a half dozen or even more varieties, preferably with different colors and bloom variations. All you have to do is to apply the pollen from one plant to the reproductive parts of another bloom (this will be called the parent plant). See photos. Looking at a Daylily bloom you will observe it has three sepals and three petals (called segments) and from out of the throat comes six stamens with the pollen-bearing tips, and one separated pistil with a stigma on top (this is the female part). The pollen bearing stamens are removed (snipped or pulled from flower) and the pollen (dust) is rubbed on the stigma of the plant you have selected as the parent and which will set seed. Apply this pollen before 11 A.M. if you want success in getting seed to set. Some certain types will set seed if pollen is applied later in the day, but for the general run of Daylilies use the early morning hours from 8 to 11 A.M. Within six weeks you should have fully ripened seed pods with 6 to 20 or even more shiny black seeds. Usually the pods will turn brown and crack open slightly at the top. They can be removed from the plant at this stage and planted immediately or saved for a few weeks. Do not save longer than 60 days, for they start losing their viability quickly.

* * * *

Some growers sow their seeds in the soil, others use mediums of all kinds. Some prefer a big tub, box or other types of containers. I use sawdust for mine, and also large tubs filled with sawdust, perlite or a mixture of vermiculite, soil and sawdust. They germinate so easily, that it doesn't make too much difference. In sawdust and perlite, they can even be set on top and not have to be covered. If planted in soil, just barely cover seeds. If planted deep, you will lose them.

WHERE TO GET DAYLILY CATALOG OR LISTS

Gilbert Wild & Son
178 Joplin St. (Catalog $1)
Sarcoxie, Mo. 64862

J. C. Dalton
Rt. 1, Box 107
Bristol, Fla. 32321

Thomasville, Nurseries
Thomasville, Ga.

* * * *

SPECIAL Note: There are literally thousands of plants, trees, seeds, blubs, etc. that cannot be found in average garden store or nursery, but may be found in the FLORIDA MARKET BULLETIN pub. every two weeks. You may place your name on the list free of charge (if resident). Write them: Market Bulletin, Mayo Bldg., Tallahassee, Fla. 32304

Blackberries Are Easy To Grow

The wild blackberry (or dewberry) that grew around the old home or farm, has been replaced by the more productive hybrids. There are three well known varieties used for commercial or home plantings. The OKLAWAHA and the FLORDAGRAND are of the trailing type and bear fruit in April and May. The BRAZO (which came from Texas) is a semi-erect type that starts to bear about time the other two are finished. It does not need cross-pollination of the trailing types. If you have limited space the Brazo is recommended. Under ideal conditions it is a heavy producer.

All three varieties should have good soil and drainage to get a high yield of fruit. When planted in rows, the trailing type are spaced from 5 to 10 feet apart. The most common type of trellis consists of three evenly spaced horizontal strands of wire, with the top one five feet high. Anchor the end posts. If needed, other posts in between may be added. Tie one cane to the TOP wire, and as the other canes develop droop them over the other wires. It is not necessary to tie the other canes, as the thorns will usually hold them in place. Do not bend canes sharply.

The semi-erect BRAZO variety should be planted 4 to 6 feet apart in the row. They do not always need a trellis. Study the photo. This planting shows a typical yard trellis with 2 feet high posts with a 2 x 4 across each end in the middle of a 10 or 12 feet length. Single strands of wire reach

Trailing types Oklawaha and Flordagrand
On single wire trellis.

the whole length. They are placed about 14 to 18 inches apart.

Blackberry plants are propagated by leafy stem cutting under mist. The stem cutting method lends itself more readily to the trailing types which sucker poorly from the roots. Cuttings can be obtained from an established plant, using the new canes while their growth is still soft. Many nurseries supply new plants ready to set out. You will also find many listed in the MARKET BULLETIN put out by the Fla. Dept. of Agriculture, Mayo Bldg. Tallahassee, Fla. 32304. (Its free to residence owners). Or write for plants to Demko Nurseries Box 38 Altoona, Fla. 32703.

After planting new plants, it is advisable to apply about 1/5 lb. per plant using 8-8-8 fertilizer applied in a uniform band 8 to 12 inches wide around the plant and from 6 to 12 inches from the plants. If planted in late Fall or Winter, do not apply any more fertilizer until late February or early March. This time use about 1/3 lb. per plant. Repeat 8 to 10 week intervals until early September. Be sure to water well during long dry spells.

After fruiting is over, cut back plants to near the ground. New ones will soon start growing for the next season. For further details, write to your County Agent, or the Agricultural Ext. Service. Inst. of Food., University of Fla., Gainesville, Fla. and ask for Circular No. 325 called Blackberry Production in Fla.

BRAZO Variety growing on low trellis

Fast Growing Trees

IN THIS DAY of speed we even expect our trees, shrubs and plants to grow faster. Atomic radiation and growth hormones and other discoveries have helped in many ways, but it still takes time to grow a fairly large tree. Nature does oblige by providing a number of trees and shrubs that would be considered as fast growing or medium-fast growing in tropical Florida and other similar areas of the world. Because so many people of retirement age settle in Florida, they naturally seek plants that will provide beauty, shade, flowers or fruit in the quickest possible time.

The term "Fast-Growing" as applied to the trees and shrubs described in these pages, means a growth of 12 feet in height within three years or from 12 to 20 feet within four or five years. This of course means that the ideal soil and care are provided. A number of trees included will even grow taller in this length of time, and some without any special soil or care. Medium-fast growing trees and shrubs are those who take one or two years longer to reach 12 feet or more. Not all trees in the list attain great heights, as some will be full grown or have reached their limits at the height of 10, 12 or 15 feet.

There are a good many trees that seem to be very slow in growth the first two or three years, then all of a sudden they shoot upward five to ten feet or more in a year. Certain families like the Bombax which incldues the Kapok (Ceiba), Shaving Brush (Pachira), Chorisia and Bombax malabaricum start slow and then attain height fairly fast after a three or four year period. The Java Plum and other Eugenias have somewhat the same characterstics.

MELALEUCA (Cajeput or Punk) Bottle Brush Tree in bloom.

Cajeput trees used for boundary of property or to line driveways or roads.

Melaleuca, Cajeput or Bottle-Brush Trees

Although we have a few native trees that are considered to be fast or medium growing, the largest number of the now popular trees in the group came from Australia, India, Africa and other parts of the world.

One of the most useful and most popular of all the fast-growing trees is called the PUNK Tree on the West Coast of Florida, MELALEUCA on the East Coast, but in proper circles it is rightly called *Melaleuca leucadendron* or even CAJE-PUT would be correct. In its native Australia it is called Cajeput. Either name is preferred to Punk Tree which gives the impression of something bad or no-good. Melaleuca (mel-a-lew-ka) is far more musical in sound, but this is only part of the botanical name.

There are many useful trees among the various Melaleucas of the world. This group and another related group called the Callistemons are commonly called "Bottle-Brush Trees" because their flowers do resemble the familiar household bottle-brush in shape and bristles. On the CAJE-PUT the flowers have long-exerted stamens of greenish-white to creamy-white color, (and have that bottle-brush shape) and are borne in pro-

Fast Growing Trees

fusion three or four times a year. These flower spikes produce many button or berry-like seed capsules that encircle the branches. After each flowering cycle is finished and the seed capsules have started to mature, an inch or more space of branch and leaves will appear, and then a new flower cycle starts. This may go on for years, however the winds and perhaps age will cause many to break off and drop to the ground. Inside of each berry-like capsule are hundreds of very minute brown seeds. If you will clip off the branches or bunches of matured pods and place them in a bag or box and leave them for three or four weeks, a mass of brown dust (these are the seeds) will be found. You may use the seeds to grow Cajeputs in wet places (not standing water) or to sow in prepared flats with soil and peat or sawdust and peat. If you have swampy areas near you, a few branches (with the seed capsules on them) laid on the wet soil will produce hundreds of seedlings that can be transplanted to cans or open ground. It is much better to raise them to at least 16 or 18 inches before setting where they are to grow. Many nurseries in Cajeput areas offer small plants in quart cans, or larger ones in big containers.

If you will bite into leaves of the Cajeput, you will detect a taste of Vicks Salve or inhalant which is similar to Eucalyptus oil. The Eucalyptus by the way is related to this tree, and both the Eucalyptus Oil and Cajeput oil are used for the same purposes. The Oil of Cajeput is much stronger according to research. A missionary to Africa once told me that the natives in certain areas planted the Cajeput very thick to keep down the mosquitos, and it does help in this respect here in Florida.

* * * *

The CAJEPUT may be considered as a flowering tree, an ornamental, a hedge or boundary tree, a windbreak, a partial shade tree, or just an effective specimen tree in singles or groups. As a flowering tree it is one of the most prolific, and very spectacular at times, especially when a large group are in bloom at the same time. There is a peculiar odor that permeates the atmosphere, and many people object to this virtue, others claim they smell like "fresh buttermilk" and don't mind it. The odor only last a few days, but the flowers will fade and persist for a week or more. One thing is sure, they certainly do attract the bees, and it is said that the Cajeput blossoms produce eight to ten times more honey than any other plant. This honey however has a very medicinal flavor, and may be used for mucous conditions of the nose and throat. If you have beehives or are a producer of orange blossom or other honeys, then it is not advisable to plant Cajeput in the vicinity. In other words, do not use this tree near orange groves, or any large plantings where honey is a business or a by-product.

For a boundary tree the Cajeput is one of the best. You may use it to outline your lot, home

grounds, or to line a drive-way. The author has over 2,000 that outline 2½ acres and also are used on both sides of a circle driveway 600 ft. long. Likewise, the tree may be used for windbreak purposes, and if used either as a boundary or windbreak they should be planted from two to three feet apart. It will take from two to three years to attain a height of 10 to 18 feet, if you start with 18 inch seedlings. Fertilizing heavily will produce the same heights in far less time. To keep them bushy, keep pinching out the terminals at frequent intervals.

Almost any fertilizer or plant food may be used for Cajeputs, but because their native habitat was the swamps or low wet places, it has been found that an Azalea or Camellia formula with extra acidity produces better results than ordinary formulas. Manures, humus, compost or organic matter also help produce lush growth. Even without any plant food or fertilizer they seem to thrive and grow in places that are considered sandy or of very little fertility. Many hundreds are grown along the seacoasts on both sides of Florida from Central Florida southward.

The CAJEPUT has many other virtues that need exploring, and no doubt it has many commercial possibilities. The wood for instance, is one of the hardest woods grown in Florida, and excellent for cabinets and furniture. There is a purplish cast to the wood when mature. The bark which is paper-like and has many thin layers has been used for insulation and has paper possibilities. The leaves and the branches are used to produce Cajeput oil.

In closing about the Cajeput, they are perhaps the most useful of all fast-growing trees for the general landscape, whether planted as a single specimen or in groups of three or more. Remember they are almost free from disease and pests. Even if hit by cold spells, they usually make a quick come-back. Most nurseries and plant stores sell them in cans, and seldom charge over 25 cents each (12 to 18 inches high).

OTHER BOTTLE-BRUSH TREES

While there are many other useful Bottle-Brush trees and shrubs that are considered fast or medium-fast growing, they do not possess all the virtues of the CAJEPUT. However, there are some that are far superior in spectacular effects. For instance the RED FLOWERING WEEPING BOTTLEBRUSH Tree is truly one of the most beautiful trees for masses of color (or even in the single cluster). There are several Red Flowering Bottlebrushes that have the weeping characteristics, and some confusion still exists as to the correct names. Menninger calls one the SHOWY BOTTLE-BRUSH and its name botanically is *Callistemon Speciosus*, however there is another that is a variation of *Callistemon citrinus* (Curt.) known as *Callistemon splendens.* This one has larger flowers of deep red but tipped with golden anthers

56

Fast Growing Trees

Red Flowering Weeping Bottlebrush

and seldom reaches over 10 feet in height. The name Callistemon viminalis has also been applied to the C. Citrinus, however some state it has wider leaves and reaches to 20 ft. in height. All of this name confusion should not keep you from enjoying one or more of the Red Flowering Bottle-brushes, and the reliable nurseries will supply them with either the proper names or maybe their own names. One thing to remember, there is still another red flowering bottle-brush that bears stiff erect branches and erect flower spikes and much larger seed carpsules (like berries) than the others. This one is *Callistemon rigidus* and more common, however very slow growing in comparison. This one grows in areas from Clearwater, Florida to the Keys, however the weeping types mentioned grow as far north as Tallahassee. All the Melaleucas and the Callistemons belong in the large Myrtle family.

YELLOW OR GOLD FLOWERING TREES

Among the fast and medium-fast growing trees there are some that bear beautiful golden or yellow flowers that enhance the landscape or garden. One of the group known as the GOLDEN RAIN TREE might as well be called The Chameleon Tree, for it changes color from a mass of gold

to delightful pinkish bracts that resemble small Japanese lanterns. Botanically this tree is known as *Koelreuteria formosana*, and it is suitable for almost any climatic conditions in Florida and all the Southern states. The large panicles of bright yellow flowers appear from September to November, depending on the section of the state in which they are grown. The Golden Rain Tree seldom exceeds 25 to 35 ft. in height, and may bloom when only 8 or 10 feet high. In good soil they will grow to 10 feet in 3 or 4 years. The foliage resembles that of the familiar Chinaberry Tree (in Florida), however it is a lighter green color. During the colder months they will drop their leaves, but not for long. Many Golden Rain Trees are found in the homes and gardens of Tampa, Florida.

They are very useful trees as specimens or groups, and may also be used as street or highway trees. Not critical about plant food requirements, any regular garden type is suitable. They don't like low wet soils, but prefer medium to medium sandy soils.

Of the yellow-flowering group, perhaps the most striking in brilliance and depth of color (gold) is the one commonly called the TREE OF GOLD. It has another common name that might cause confusion or confliction, because it is the "SILVER TRUMPET" tree. The word silver refers to the silver-gray leaves, or it might even refer to the light-gray corky bark.

If we must have a common name, then the TREE OF GOLD would seem more appropiate.

Cassia fistula . . . Golden Shower

Fast Growing Trees

The botanical name is *Tabebuia argentea*. It is a fast growing tree in ideal soil or location, but only a medium-fast grower when grown in the colder areas where they are often set-back for a year or more. They are well suited for Pinellas county southward and likewise for same latitude on the East Coast. The Sarasota to Naples section of the West Coast of Florida has many outstanding trees. They come into their glory about the latter part of March into April or perhaps a few weeks later. This tree is a favorite to attach orchids or hanging baskets to, because of its wide-furrowed cork-like bark and curved graceful branches. Seldom exceeds 25 feet in height. Leaves may, or may not be present when the flowers a r e in bloom. Likes fairly rich soil, but must have good drainage. Propagation from seeds, cuttings or air-layering. There are a number of Tabebuias that bear pink (*Tab. pallida*) or *Tab. pentaphyllia*, or some with tinges of rose color (*Tab. rosea*) and even others with yellow flowers. From Palm Beach southward you will find quite a variety of these beautiful trees, however not all as fast growing as the Tree of Gold.

* * * *

The GOLDEN SHOWER is another common name for a gold or yellow-flowering tree of an entirely different family. This one, *Cassia fistula* is perhaps one of the best known of yellow-flowering trees in fast or medium growing category. It bears long dangling chains of fairly large, fragrant light yellow to golden yellow flowers that appear from May to July and vary considerably with the individual tree, the weather and the location. Following the flowers, long tube-like seed pods form (and this accounts for the Latin name fistula which means tube or pipe) and in certain parts of the world they are used in medicines or for laxatives. Senna comes from the pods of the Golden Shower and other Cassias. In Florida the Golden Shower is used mainly for specimen trees in the home grounds, along the street or they are ideal for parks, estates, etc. I would put them in the medium-fast growing category.

Average tree attains 30 to 35 feet in height, but may go another 10 ft. in ideal soil and location. Likes good drainage and fairly rich soil. Not suitable above Vero Beach or Homosassa Springs. Does very well in Pinellas and Hillsborough Counties southward. Propagation mainly from seeds, but air-layering has been used with moderate success. There are many more Cassias that do well in the same areas that bear yellow, pink or rose colored flowers. *Cassia beareana, siamea, bi-capsularis,* are suitable for the colder areas of the state. Among the pink or rose colored Cassias suitable for the warmer areas, are *Cassia nodosa, javanica, renigera, grandis,* all of which are medium fast growing types.

* * * *

Another very useful yellow-flowering tree that reaches 10 to 20 feet in height and blooms in the Spring and again in the Fall is one that is commonly called the YELLOW ELDER or *Tecoma stans* of the *Bignonia* family. It is a low-branching tree with bright green foliage with drooping clusters of yellow fragrant flowers of funnel-form shape. The individual flowers have a pale green calyx with the throat being delicately etched in orange shades. The leaves are the tapering type with serrated edges and range from two to seven inches long. While the Yellow Elder will grow in a variety of soils, it must have good drainage and will not stand wet feet. Very well suited for the seacoast or inland from Central Florida southward. Some are even grown in protected areas of North Florida. Easily propagated from seeds which are plentiful after each blooming cycle. If you have room, plant one or more Yellow Elders for beauty of form and flowers, and as an eye-stopper.

The SILK OAK or AUSTRALIAN SILK OAK tree produces some of the most unusual flowers of all the trees mentioned, and they might be classified as deep gold, bronze or even orange-yellow. While this tree is not usually classified as a flowering tree, I see no reason why it doesn't rate in this category. One thing however is certain, it does grow fairly fast and will reach 80 to 100 feet in time. Average tree height would probably be about 40 feet in 8 to 10 years. Another thing is certain, it is not an oak tree or even related to the oak family. Botanically it is *Grevillea robusta* (Proteaceae family). The foliage however might have some resemblance to certain oaks, and maybe accounts for the common name Silk Oak. The leaves are silvery on the underside, or some may say they are silky in appearance. Wind-blown foliage does give a silky or silvery effect that makes it an ideal landscape tree. The foliage drops at intervals during the colder months, and sometimes it is completely leafless, however certain trees may have foliage the entire year.

Grevillea robusta growth is more or less straight and is an ideal timber tree, but seldom

Close-up of blossoms on Australian Silk Oak Tree (Grevillea robusta). Deep bronze or gold color.

Fast Growing Trees

used for this purpose in Florida. Reports claim it is actually termite-proof. Perhaps this tree may become a good commercial item in Florida in the near future. Propagates from seeds, cuttings and air-layering.

The RED SILK OAK (*Grevillea banksii*) which bears very beautiful deep-red blossoms is an ideal lawn specimen or garden tree that seldom exceeds 10 or 12 feet, but may go to 20 feet in ideal soils and locations. Its foliage is very silky and lacey, slightly larger than *Gre. robusta*. Not suitable for the colder areas of Central Florida, but does well from Bradenton southward. Fairly fast growing.

* * * *

There are a number of Acacias that are among the fast growing trees, and which bear yellow flowers. The EAR-LEAF ACACIA or *Acacia auriculiformis* is one that has beautiful form and very dense foliage. The leaves (phyllodes) are long and narrow and slightly curved or sickle-shaped. In the Spring and sometimes at other times during the year the yellow but not too conspicuous flower-clusters appear, and are followed by grayish seed-pods which curve and twist and have some resemblance to the human ear. The small round almost black seeds are used to start most of the Ear-Leaf Acacias. This is one of the better fast growing trees for general use in the landscape, and for density of foliage. Average height is 25 to 30 feet and occasionally to 40 feet. Also a good windbreak tree. Suited for lower Central and South Florida areas.

A closely related tree the *Acacia longifolia* (known as the SYDNEY GOLDEN WATTLE) is also a fast growing tree to be used in the same manner as the Ear-Leaf Tree. This bears yellowish catkin-like flowers in loose spikes followed by seed pods up to 5 inches long.

There are many other fine Acacias that grow fairly fast and produce yellow flowers, or puffball yellow flowers and suited for same areas as those described. Some have ferny foliage with thorns (such as *Acacia farnesiana* which is also called *Popinac or Opopanax*). The BULL-HORN Acacia (*Acacia cornigera*) has really vicious thorns (inflated) that resemble those of an ox or bull and sometimes reach three inches in length. Hundreds of small pincushion-like yellow flowers appear during the year. This one planted mainly as a novelty or to keep people and animals out of the area.

The JERUSALEM THORN tree as its name indicates, is graced with many spines or thorns, but it is a quick-growing ornamental flowering tree which has a sort of misty-green appearance (especially in Spring). Produces bright yellow flowers in Spring and sometimes in the Fall. The flowers are slightly fragrant and are followed by seed pods of brownish color from one to five inches long. The leaves of this tree are sometimes a foot long and have numerous small segments. The correct name is *Parkinsonia aculeata*, but more com-monly called just Parkinsonia. Will reach to 30 feet and suitable for almost all areas of Florida. Easily started from seeds.

FLOWERING AND NON-FLOWERING FAST GROWING TREES

A tree with exceptional beauty of form and foliage that is not too well known is one known as the MALAYAN ALMOND or *Terminalia muelleri*. Although this one and others are called Tropical Almond trees, they are not to be confused with the true or edible almond trees that produce the nuts found in candy bars, etc. The Malayan Almond tree will reach the height of 12 to 15 feet within three years from seed. It grows in tiers and each year a new one is added, and soon it assumes a very symmetrical shape that makes it very outstanding in the landscape. The leaves range from two to four inches long and are obtuse or abruptly pointed, slightly hairy underneath. If you have a cold spell or two that is not too severe, the foliage takes on many colors of yellow, ochre, orange, red, wine or maroon. The nice part of this change, is that they remain nearly all Winter and sometimes right into the early Spring. They are seldom leafless. Should this occur, it is just for a week or more. The Spring foliage is truly a beautiful green, and many hundreds of upright flower spikes appear. The flowering may continue all Summer, and they have a peculiar odor that is not unpleasant, but not exactly fragrant. The fruit or nut that follows has a dark purple color with a slight down. It is fleshy, but with a large seed. They average about ¾ of an inch long and are responsible for many seedlings that come up under the tree. These seedlings may be transplanted easily when about 3 or 4 inches high, but do not wait for any more growth, for they form a long tap-root after five inches or more. *Terminalia muelleri* is ideal for that curve in the driveway or road or anywhere in the landscape where you want form, color and medium shade.

The so called TROPICAL ALMOND or Florida Almond Tree is better known than the Malayan Almond, and it is used much in the same manner. This one is *Terminalia catappa* and its fruit are much larger. They are huge in comparison and are greenish to red in color. Likewise the foliage is different, being large shiny leaves that give more density to the tree, and without the tier fashion of growing.

Both the Malayan and the Tropical Almond trees are suited for lower Central and all of South Florida.

For the same area as the Tropical Almonds, there is a quick-growing tree known as PONGAMIA which attains 25 to 40 feet in 5 or 6 years. Pea-like white, pink or lavender flowers hang in clusters similar to the Wisteria. Flat broad seed pods with a little hooked beak on the end and each carrying one kidney-shaped seed appear all over the tree. An oil called POONGA oil is obtained from the seeds, and is used by natives of

Fast Growing Trees

Malaya for medicine, lighting, and antiseptics. The Pongamia pinnata tree is very ornamental, a good shade tree, and useful for windbreaks or for highway planting. Sheds many leaves during the year, but they are renewed in April and May. Propagated mainly from seeds. Likes good drainage.

Another of the thorny trees that is a fairly fast growing tree is one called PITHECOLOBIUM or Monkey Pod Tree. It has very unusual bluish-green foliage. Although the tree is good for shade, ornament, and for food for monkeys, it is not a tree to climb because of the many sharp spines along the trunk and branches. Flowers are white in dense heads, but not conspicuous. The fruit or seed pods range from 4 to 6 inches in length and are spirally twisted. In Mexico it is often called the Mexican St. Johns Bread Tree. Personally, I will leave this food for the monkeys. The *Pithecolobium dulce* becomes a fairly large tree in the dryer types of soil (not sandy) and may reach to 50 feet in time. The average tree in South Florida is from 25 to 35 feet in height. A few years ago it was attacked by thorn-bugs which did a lot of damage, however these pests do not show up every year.

* * * *

The MOTHER'S TONGUE Tree is one of the fastest growing trees from seed of all so far, and it is one with many uses. Some people regard it as a nuisance, on account of the many flat seed pods that cover the landscape for 60 days or more in the early Spring. If you are not inclined to utilize all waste products of plants and trees, then it may be a tree to avoid, but on the other hand if you want its wonderful honey-suckle fragrance at three or four intervals during the year, and its beautiful form and greenish color, then plant one or more *Albizzia lebbek* or Mother's Tongue Trees. Being a leguminous tree, it is reported that nearly all plants in the vicinity of its roots do better. Some even claim that Citrus bears better when these trees are planted among the grove at regular intervals. A dairyman states that his cows gave more milk when they could eat the foliage and exposed roots of the Mother's Tongue tree. From personal experience the author knows that the seed pods make one of the finest of mulches when piled up for a period of three or four months and when it is composted with manures, humus, garbage, etc. You may pile them in a barrel or bin and give them a good wetting now and then, and they are ready to use in a short time.

It is another tree with commercial possibilites, for it makes an excellent timber tree with a very hard dark brown hardwood. It will grow in a variety of soils from high sandy to richer dark soils.

Mother's Tongue Tree is suited for lower Central and all of South Florida. You will find nearly all the seedlings you need under an established tree or nearby. Nurseries very seldom sell plants because they are so plentiful.

The Mother's Tongue Tree has a much hardier sister that grows in much colder climates than Florida, but is well suited for all of Florida except the extreme southern tips. This tree is *Albizzia julibrissin* or better known by the common name of MIMOSA. The Mimosa is one of the main flowering and shade trees of North Florida and most parts of Central Florida. The Jacksonville to Gainesville district has many thousands of trees that are a beautiful sight during the Summer and sometimes into the Fall. The flowers range from light to deep pink and are almost identical with the Mother's Tongue in make-up and appearance. Mimosa foliage is smaller than Mother's Tongue tree. Seed pods are brown when mature, very flat and from 4 to 6 inches long. Starts easily from seed, however this tree is not as fast in growth as *Albizzia lebbek*. May also be started from root cuttings. Reaches to 30 or 40 feet in height, and assumes a symmetrical more or less drooping form. Does well in almost any soil where there is good drainage.

The *Hibiscus tiliaceus or Hibiscus elatus* trees commonly called the MAHOE or MAHOE HIBISCUS Trees are among the fastest growing of big leaf trees. These are covered in the chapter on Hibiscus relatives.

* * * *

AUSTRALIAN PINES is a familiar name in almost all areas of Florida, and they rate as one of the fastest growing trees for windbreaks, to stop soil erosion in sandy areas along the seacoast, or as highway trees. For many years they were used for street trees all over Florida, and many shaped them into hedges of all descriptions. They also lined the highways on both sides through the Everglades and Tamiami Trail. One lesson however has been learned, and that is they have such a tremendous root system that they uproot sidewalks, highways, septic tanks and many other items nearby. During the worst of hurricanes in the Everglades they blew across the roadways and became a hazard. Because of their fast growth and tremendous heights, the trimmings and pruning became too costly, so the planting of Australian Pines was prohibited. Nevertheless, they are useful trees in wide open spaces where windbreak protection is helpful, and along the sandy beaches to help hold the soil.

The AUSTRALIAN PINE is not actually a pine tree, or even a member of the pine family. They are rightfully called Casuarinas. The name refers to the resemblance of the drooping feathers of the Cassowary bird which is a native of Australia. There are a number of Casuarinas that are suitable for Florida, however only three are grown in abundance. The one referred to as the horsetail trees is *Casuarina equisetifolia*. Another one is called *Casuarina cunninghamiana* or Cunningham Pine (and it is not a pine). This one will grow in the colder areas of Florida and in South

Fast Growing Trees

Georgia, but will stand the salt-air of the coast like Cas. equisetifolia (also called the the Beef-wood tree). The third one is called *Casuarina lepidophloia*, and is better for windbreak or hedge use because of its thicker foliage. Does not set seed in Florida, so must be propagated from root suckers which sprout freely under the trees. Nearly all the Casuarinas will reach to 70 even a 100 feet in height. Small cones are collected from the first two of the list and put in a box and seeds will drop out, or are easily removed in a very short time.

* * * *

The CHINESE TALLOW Tree (*Sapium sebiferum*) is one of the fast growing trees suitable for nearly all areas of Florida and particularly the Central and Northern parts. Has a spreading habit of growth and will reach to 30 feet within five years in good soil. The poplar-like leaves go through many Autumn changes of color. An ideal tree for specimens or shade, and practically free of disease and pests. Milk-white seeds, with three to the capsule, are borne in profusion and adhere to the central column of the capsule for weeks after opening. In China the waxy coating is used for candle and soap making. In the same family as the Poinsettia or Euphorbiaceae family. No cultural requirements. Very hardy and colorful tree.

* * * *

The JAMBOLAN or JAVA PLUM Tree probably would be rated as number one among the fast growing trees started from seed and would take first place for surety of germination of every seed that touches soil. The author came across several trees in Laurel, Fla. about 1949 and from seeds and small trees obtained from Paul Melroy and the late Col. Wm. R. Grove, I have helped popularize this tree in Pinellas and Hillsborough Counties to the extent that there are many hundreds now growing and some have reached 60 to 70 feet in height. The first seeds I planted produced a growth of 20 feet within three years, and bore fruit at four and five years of age. Although this tree is not actually a plum in the botanical sense, the fruit is as tart as most plums and may be used for making wonderful jellies, jams, and wine. Most trees produce so much fruit that the majority of it goes to waste. The fruit is elongated and shaped similar to an olive and will average from one inch to an inch and a half long. When ripe it is dark purple with a very juicy white and purple flesh and a fairly large seed. As fresh fruit, it is useful, but only appeals to certain people. Some like the first bite, others cultivate a taste for them. The fruit varies with the individual trees, some being very sweet when fully ripe, others have a bit of astringency. The fruiting season varies with weather conditions and also individual trees. Usually the first ripe fruits come in latter part of May and often you find ripe fruit as late as September. The flowering season starts in February or March and as late as April. Flowers are usually borne on the old wood, and in branched auxilliary clusters and are a dingy white and not very conspicuous. Fruits hang in clusters like grapes.

The Java Plum is classified as either *Eugenia jambolana or cumini*, however some claim it is *Syzygium jambolana or cumini*. It is related to the Surinam Cherry, Rose Apple (*Eug. jambos*), *Eug. Hookeriana*, and quite a few other tropical fruits in this classification. Most of the Eugenias came from Java, Ceylon and India, and have been fairly well established in South and lower Central Florida.

By habit of growth the Java Plum (or Jambolan) will usually fill all the intervening space from the ground to the top. The branches are rubbery and able to stand very heavy winds without breaking. During some of the worst hurricanes along the East Coast of Florida they proved their value as windbreaks and specimen trees. After the trees are about three years old, you may prune the lower parts, or shape it any way you desire. I have seen a hedge 15 feet high and a block long near Boynton Beach, Fla.

You never know, when you plant a seed, just how many trunks the tree will have in a few years. Some keep only one trunk, others may have from two to eight. Another wonderful virtue of this tree is its ability to go through hard-pan with its root system. They will even thrive at the edge of salt marshes. They grow fast in almost any ordinary soil, but still faster in low, wet or mucky soils.

A cold spell will often set small trees back for a period, and even touch the big ones, but most make a wonderful come-back if cold spells are not too severe and frequent.

Insects rarely bother the Java Plum, however they are sometimes subject to whiteflies that

JAVA PLUM FRUIT Small to large clusters are produced.

cause sooty mold on leaves. It has been my experience that the constant renewing of foliage will overcome most of the sooty mold. Personally, I use all the leaves that drop for mulching roses, daylilies, all kinds of shrubs and trees. They do as well as oak leaves for Azaleas and Camellias.

For dense shade, windbreaks, and boundary trees the Jambolan is ideal. Its main objection has been the abundance of fruit that drops to the ground for several months. We rake them up and use them in compost after the jelly-making is over.

The Australian Brush Cherry Tree or *Eugenia Hookeriana* is likewise a fast growing tree with smaller foliage, but with clusters of pinkish to rose colored fruits that are round. Fruit is edible but very mild. Makes a beautiful colored mild jelly. Grows fast from seed, but not nearly as fast as Java Plum, and reaches only to 25 or 30 feet in height.

* * * *

The word FICUS means fig, however not all Ficus trees bear the type of figs we are accustomed to eating. Over 600 species of Ficus are scattered over the Old and New World, and many of them are mentioned in the Bible. The sycamore fruit that Amos gathered was a fig named *Ficus sycamorus*. Even the familiar Rubber Tree or the big Banyan trees are fig or Ficus trees. In Florida there are perhaps a hundred or more Ficus trees, but for discussion on fast-growing trees we will include only one or two of the real popular general landscape types.

The INDIAN LAUREL or *Ficus nitida* (now classed as *Ficus retusa*) is perhaps one of the most common and one of the fastest growing of the Ficus in Florida. The late Dr. Henry Nehrling states that only a poet-naturalist can do justice to this most elegant, graceful and noble species. "Never have I seen a tree so ideally beautiful, so densely deep green, so noble in aspect and growth." Adding to his remarks I would like to say that the dark green foliage is glossy, forms a very compact head and almost a pyramidal shape, and grows very fast, and is very hardy in lower Central and all of South Florida. It is attacked by thrips in some localities but new growth often overtakes the damage. It may be sprayed with such formulas as ISOTOX Garden Spray and others. Some nurseries offer thrip-proof varieties.

The LOFTY FIG or *Ficus altissima* is another rapid growing tree, but needs plenty of space to expand in years to come. Some call it the Banyan Tree, and it is similar, but never attains the vast proportions of the tree best known as the Banyan or *Ficus benghalensis*. The Lofty Fig has some aerial roots, but few in comparison to the true Banyan mentioned. Its large leathery leaves are a glossy green, rounded and beautifully veined with white. The fruits which usually mature about April are dotted, reddish within and about 3/8 inch across. A favorite of the birds, I don't advise using *Ficus altissima* unless you have plenty of room.

There are a good many Ficus trees and vines that are just as well adapted for area, but space does not allow us to cover them. In closing, perhaps you would like to know that the edible figs or Ficus sold on the market are *Ficus carica* Most of the dried figs are raised in California or the Holy Land. In Florida you can raise very fine Black, Brown, Brunswick, Celeste, Green Ischia, Lemon, and other named varieties that grow fast and produce very delicious figs for fresh consumption. They like clay soils of Central and North Florida, but will grow in other areas if a heavy one-foot mulch and plenty of humus is used. Some use iron filings, old steel wool, and such in the planting holes. Colloidal phosphate mixed with chicken manure and compost is also recommended.

* * * *

AUNT CLIFF'S JAVA PLUM JELLY

The Jambolan fruit (Java Plum) makes extra fine jelly with a grape color. Flavor reminds some of berry jelly, others say it is more like grape jelly.

Ingredients

4 cups of Juice	6½ cups of Sugar
½ cup Lemon Juice	Certo

Directions

Gather and wash fruit. Use a large kettle . . . bring water to 1½ inches below fruit level. Let boil 30 to 45 minutes until fruit breaks open and turns a light pink color. Crush with a potato masher and strain through heavy cloth.

Mix juices and sugar and bring to a rolling boil. Add one-half bottle of CERTO, bring back to boiling point and boil one minute. Pour into sterilized jars and seal or cover with about one-quarter inch paraffin wax.

JAVA PLUM (Eugenia Jamobolana) or Jambolan Tree

Citrus for the Garden

NEARLY EVERY FAMILY or person that makes Florida their permanent or part-time home is usually interested in growing a few fruits of the Citrus family in the yard or garden. The orange and the grapefruit are the most popular of all Citrus for general purposes; the lemon and lime come next. The Calomondin and Kumquat are extremely popular for ornamental use, or for the making of preserves, conserves, marmalades and to some extent the juice is used to make pies, drinks and punch.

ORANGE VARIETIES

There are enough orange varieties to extend the fruiting season to almost every month of the year. They are generally classified as early, mid-season and late varieties. Among the early varieties is one called PARSON BROWN which bears fairly large fruit that contains from 10 to 19 seeds each. Coarse-textured flesh filled with deep yellow juice. Peel is slightly rough and pebbly, and has a tendency to remain dark green until late in the Fall. Parson Brown ripening period is mostly in October and November. It is a very vigorous and upright grower and quite resistant to cold, making it suitable for the fringe areas as well as the regular Citrus belt. The HAMLIN is another popular early orange with very smooth fine-textured skin. Fruit is slightly oval and contains from one to five seeds each. Its sweetness is developed early in the Fall. Not as cold resistant as the Parson Brown variety. Hamlin oranges should never be sprayed with Lime-sulphur during Summer or Fall months.

* * * *

Midseason oranges include two extremely popular varieties known as the PINEAPPLE and the TEMPLE orange. The PINEAPPLE variety is noted for the deep red color of its peel and the rich flavor of its juice. Each orange contains from 12 to 20 seeds. Pineapples are the most widely grown of all oranges.

The TEMPLE ORANGE is the favorite of many, and is rapidly taking number one place for quality. It is medium in size, oblate, and usually tapers slightly to the stem end. Peel has deep red color and is easily separated. Flesh is also a deep red color with a decidedly different flavor and aroma than other oranges. Averages about 20 seeds per orange. The Temple Orange is actually a hybrid between a tangerine-like Citrus called the Mandarin Orange and a Sweet Orange. They ripen later than most midseason oranges, and are usually the first for the Christmas trade. This is one of the finest dooryard and grove Citrus for your consideration.

The HOMOSASSA Orange is one of the large-fruited midseason varieties with a good flavor, but with fairly coarse flesh and peel. Fruit has orange-yellow color and contains from 20 to 24 seeds.

The JAFFA ORANGE is another large midseason variety, with an orange-red peel. Flavor is excellent and produces abundant juice with good flavor. Very few seeds, with average being from 6 to 9. The Jaffa orange came from Palestine originally, but does well in most Citrus areas of Florida.

It is quite resistant to cold, and is usually preferred over the Homosassa as a dooryard tree.

* * * *

The main late crop of oranges in Florida come from VALENCIA variety. This is one of the most vigorous and cold resistant oranges for either home or commercial growing. The fruit of the Valencia is slightly oval, medium to large in size and with a deep orange color when fully ripe. Seeds are usually few in number, and seldom over six per orange. Juice is abundant and of very excellent quality. Valencia oranges extend over a long period, with shipments from March through July and sometimes later. There may be some difference in Valencias, for it is said that originally some came into Florida and California from the English nursery and that in the course of time there has been some noticeable differences.

The LUE GIM GONG is considered one of the later introductions of late bearing oranges, and it is said to have even a longer season than the Valencia, however some claim it is hard to tell one from the other. Anyway, whether Valencia or Lue Gim Gong, both are excellent for dooryard planting.

SOME MISCELLANEOUS VARIETIES

Sweet orange varieties have been divided into three groups which include the common oranges, the blood oranges, and those with the label NAVEL oranges. A number of Navel oranges have been tried in Florida and some have proven worthy of planting as a dooryard tree. It is best to consult a specialist in citrus stock before buying Navel oranges, as many sold are not of good quality. SURPRISE NAVEL is a medium-sized orange without protruding navel. The WASHINGTON NAVEL is perhaps one of the best known, but not recommended for Florida. It has a tendency to dry pulp and not very juicy.

Under favorable conditions many of the Navels are good enough for the market, but if you have limited space, better try some of the other types. BLOOD ORANGES have blood-red streaks in the

Citrus for the Garden

flesh and for this reason are known by this name. Perhaps the best of the group is known as RUBY BLOOD. It is medium to small, round to oblong orange with fairly deep red peel. Seeds number 10 to 12. Blood oranges are strictly dooryard varieties and seldom found on the regular market.

* * * *

MANDARIN oranges which are called tangerines by many people, are a group with loose fitting skin (peel) that is generally of a fine smooth texture. One known as the D A N C Y TANGERINE is not only a good dooryard tree, but one of commercial importance. Deep orange-red fruit with a nippled base and from 11 to 14 sections, and with a rich spicy flavor. They are very prolific, producing oblate fruit that average 2½ to 3 inches in lateral diameter. Seeds average about 14 each. This is one of the best.

One of the later tangerines (or Mandarin) is called the MURCOTT orange and produces very sweet fruit. Useful to extend the season. Others found on the market (sold by most nurseries) include ONECO, CLEMENTINE, a n d CLEOPATRA. Many times you hear the Mandarin group referred to as SATSUMAS, however this is really a group of varieties of Japanese origin and have the appearance in shape of the Dancy Tangerine but without the beautiful bright and deep reds. Satsumas are not highly colored, but do have wonderful flavor that is not as spicy as most Mandarins. They are grown mostly in North Central and Northern fringes of the state. Trees are dwarf nature in comparison to others, and have a tendency towards willowy growth. Best known variety of Satsumas is the OWARI.

A dooryard tree found occasionally that appears to be a large Tangerine is perhaps the KING ORANGE. This one produces fruit 3½ to 4 inches round and with a deep red colored flesh. Flavor is good and is more like an orange than a tangerine. It is grown mostly as a novelty or for collections.

* * * *

There are a number of hybrids between the Mandarin (tangerine) orange and the grapefruit. One of the best is called the TANGELO, and there are several good varieties for dooryard planting. MINEOLA TANGELO is one of the richest flavored Tangelos. It is slightly larger than the orange. Others include the ORLANDO, SEMINOLE and SAMPSON. All are good for home consumption, however the Sampson is better for rootstocks.

THE GRAPEFRUIT VARIETIES

The grapefruit has established itself everywhere as a breakfast fruit, however its juice and segments are used for all meals and in between snacks. It ranks next to the orange in popularity and in general sales. Grapefruit makes an ideal fruit tree for the yard or garden, however there is not a wide variety to choose from in comparison to that of the orange.

One of the oldest varieties in Florida is the DUNCAN, although there are a number of others with such names as McCarty, Hall, Excelsior, Walters, and Silver Cluster and which are so much alike it is hard to tell one from the other. Grove owners and packing houses now call all seedy grapefruit (or common grapefruit) the DUNCAN variety. This and other common ones average from 30 to 60 seeds each.

The seedless grapefruit that is considered the best on all counts is one called the MARSH SEEDLESS. This one does have a few seeds, and comes in white, pink or ruby flesh types. The pink or ruby flesh seedless variations are often sold as the THOMPSON, RUBY or WEBB varieties.

Although the pink or ruby-fleshed varieties are preferred by the general public, the canners of juice prefer the Duncan or comon seedy varieties for flavor. For a dooryard, either is suitable.

* * * *

Many homegrounds and gardens in Florida have large-fruited citrus which are related to the grapefruit, but called the PUMMELO or the SHADDOCK. They have very little juice, a very thick rind, flesh has a resinous or turpentine flavor. Orientals prefer them to the better grapefruit. For dooryard planting they are quite attractive and more or less a novelty fruit to attract attention.

Calomondin and Eureka Lemon

Citrus for the Garden

KEY LIMES

LEMONS AND LIMES

Although the largest majority of smooth-skinned lemons are produced in California, Spain and Sicily, there are a number of varieties of smooth and rough skin types that are suitable for dooryard planting in Florida. The most common and perhaps the best for this purpose is the VILLAFRANCA Lemon, which has excellent flavor and is very juicy. Another very good dooryard lemons is one called the MEYER LEMON. It is a more or less dwarf type of tree and the fruit is almost round. The fruit should be gathered while green and allowed to color before using—one of the hardiest of lemons for home planting. If you want another fruit tree that attracts attention, then include the PONDEROSA LEMON which produces fruit large enough to make six lemon pies each. It is an extremely acid fruit suitable for home consumption. Often the tree and fruit is mistaken for the CITRON *Citrus Medica L.*, which has a thick rind, but little juice. The Citron is another popular dooryard tree in Florida, but its fruit is seldom used. The candied citron used in fruit-cakes, candies, etc., is made in Mediterranean countries. Lemons are classified botanically as *Citrus Limon* (L.)

* * * *

LIMES are an important fruit in Florida, both commercially and for home planting. They belong in citrus species classified as *Citrus aurantifolia Swingle*. The small acid lime grown in the keys is called the KEY LIME in Florida and the West Indies, however the same lime is called Mexican lime in Mexico and Dominica in the Dominican Republic. It is a small seedy lime which is almost round, with a slight nipple. Color is light green to lemon yellow. Skin is very smooth. Juice is exceptionally good flavor and very acid, in fact it contains from 7 to 8 % citric acid. Good source of Vitamin C. Very good tree for dooryard planting. Seldom reaches over 12 to 15 feet in height and is very bushy.

The TAHITI or PERSIAN LIME is another favorite for dooryard planting or for commercial groves. This one produces large oval fruit that average about three inches long, and with a very smooth skin, green pulp and almost seedless. Juice is very acid, but of good quality. Trees seldom exceed 12 to 15 feet and are somewhat droopy in appearance. Main season is late Summer and Fall. Very popular lime for making concentrate. Do not plant either lime above lower Central Florida areas.

ORNAMENTAL CITRUS

For the homegrounds there is nothing in the Citrus or related families that equals the KUMQUAT or the CALOMONDIN for beauty, ease of growing, and continous bearing of fruit. These two small fruits are used in the yard or garden mainly for their color. When they are loaded with fruit which are orange or vermillion shades, they look like trees that have been dressed up with ornaments. During the Holidays, or anytime fruit is in season, it is more or less a custom to decorate boxes of oranges and grapefruit (shipped to friends or relatives, etc.) with a number of fruit clusters of either the Calomondin or Kumquat.

The Calomondin is an excellent substitute for lemon or lime in ice tea, and makes a delicious drink used alone or with other Citrus juices. Try making a pie of Calomondin juice and you will find it equal, if not better than a lemon pie. Use a trifle more juice for the pie than you do with lemons. The Calomondin and the Kumquat are excellent for marmalades and conserves. The fruit

NAGAMI KUMQUAT — Used for ornament in landscape or may be used to make preserves, or conserves.

Citrus for the Garden

of the Calomondin is round and shaped like a tangerine, but not much larger than a marble or cherry. It is perhaps a hybrid between a sour mandarin and a kumquat. Tree grows fairly tall and has beautiful small foliage. Most are started from seed, however some excellent ones found in nurseries are grafted.

Actually the KUMQUAT does not belong to the genus Citrus, but to a closely related genus known as Fortunella. There are several varieties in cultivation, but the main ones found on the market include the NAGAMI KUMQUAT which bears larger oval fruit, and the MARUMI KUMQUAT which bears small round fruit and is mainly used for ornamental use.

GENERAL CITRUS PLANTING AND CULTURE

For light sandy soils of Florida, rough lemon stock is used for understock. This makes it possible for trees to compete with surrounding shrubbery. The Sour Orange or the Cleopatra mandarin are used in poorly drained spots, however these stocks will not stand much competition from nearby trees and shrubs.

For young trees, it is best to plant either in the semi-dormant months of January and February or in June before the rainy season starts. Prepare the planting hole ahead of time, and allow enough space for the roots to spread out freely. Usual rule—trees should be set at same depth as they were in the nursery. It is customary to puddle the soil around tree, to keep it from sinking after it is planted. Use about 2 pounds of steamed bone meal (never use raw bone meal) mixed in with soil that is packed around the roots.

Most grove owners cut the trees down to about 12 inches when planted, however for home planting leave some of the top. Allow a space of 12 to 15 feet for oranges and grapefruit trees, and a trifle more for kumquats and calomondins.

If you plant in areas subject to cold spells, it is best to bank each tree above the bud union for the first two or three years. As soon as frost danger is past, remove the embanked soil.

FERTILIZING CITRUS

The feeding schedule for Citrus whether dooryard or grove, is Jan.-Feb., May-June—and Oct.-Nov. or in other words three times a year. Most reliable brands of fertilizers include a formula known as Citrus Specials, and which contains the right proportion of nitrogen, phosphorous, potash, and other additions such as magnesium, manganese, copper and boron. The rule covering the right amount to use for each tree is as follows; use one pound of fertilizer for each year of the tree's age up to 10 years, and for each added year, increase the amount by one-half pound. Spread the fertilizer out from the trunk to the "drip-circle" of the tree. If your lawn grows right up to the tree, then you will have to punch holes (about 6 or 8 inches deep) in the area covered. Some use the spade pushed down to the

hilt, and fill with fertilizer and then pushed back as much as possible. Applying dry fertilizer to the grass area may burn the grass, unless it is thoroughly watered after application. It is customary to supplement root feeding with nutritional sprays applied to the foliage. This supplies many of the minor elements needed for good color of foliage and better production of fruit. It also aids the flavor. Iron chelates such as SEQUESTRENE are useful for correcting iron deficiency. Minorel is another useful foliage spray.

Supplementing dry types of fertilizers for dooryard Citrus, some prefer to use one of the newer liquid fertilizers such as NA-CHURS, whereby you can feed your trees through the foliage at any time of the year. This type can also be used with a device known as a ROOT-FEEDER which is attached to the garden hose.

SPRAYING CITRUS

Large citrus groves use power equipment for applying spray mixtures, however for the dooryard planting, this would be impractical. If you have several trees, then it might pay to buy one of the portable pressure sprayers. There are a number of hose attachments that will take small amounts of spray mixtures, and the same item may be used for all your shrubs and trees. The ORTHO firm makes such items, and another is the GRO-GUN. Ask your dealer.

Most of the damage done by pests is caused by Florida Red Scale which appear as little red, slightly conical, circular spots on leaves and fruit, and the Purple Scale which are crusty, sort of wedged-shaped, immobile insects about $1/8$ inch, and found on twigs and leaves, and also on the fruit that touches foliage, etc. Both of these scales may be controlled by an oil emulsion such as Florida Volck or Linoil. Use five tablespoonfuls to each gallon of water. Time to apply is June or July.

Other pests include the Aphids, which are greenish or brownish plant lice that attack the young growth and cause new leaves to curl, and the tiny mothlike Whiteflies which are abundant, especially on the underside of leaves. It is their flat oval green larvae that do the real damage. Whiteflies cause the black sooty mold on top of leaves. They secrete a honey-dew that causes the mold to spread. Ants also cause the spreading of mold. For both Aphids and Whiteflies use Nicotine Sulphate solution such as Black Leaf 40. This can be mixed with the oil emulsion spray at the rate of one teaspoonful to the gallon. You may use RETOX or ISOTOX for the same purpose. A detergent such as Joy can be added to the mixture as a wetting and spreading agent.

Yellow Rust mites which are almost invisible, produce greasy spots on leaves and cause them to drop, and also cause a slick brown "russeting" on the fruit. Give a sulphur dusting every six weeks from blooming until fruit ripens.

Lychees

THE DRIED FORM of Lychee fruits have been sold or served in Chinatown stores and restaurants of some of our big cities like New York, Chicago and San Francisco for many years. American born Orientals and others call them "lee-chee nuts." This however is incorrect on two scores. First, they are not a nut (a large seed within is not edible) and secondly, the correct name in areas of China where they are grown on a large scale is Lychee (pronounced lie-chee). Even the botanical name is *Lit-chi chinensis*.

* * *

Not many people in this country were acquainted with the fresh lychee fruit until the late Col. Wm. R. Grove Sr., proved they could be grown as a commercial crop or as a dooryard tree in certain areas of Florida. Retiring from the Army at 65 years of age, he settled in Laurel, Fla. which is 14 miles south of Sarasota. There in 1938 he planted his first Lychee trees. He also discovered a method of quick propagation of new trees using plastics and peat moss, and which he patented under the name of AIRWRAP method of air-layering of plants. (See section on propagation). Col. Grove was not the first man to plant a lychee tree in Florida, but he was responsible for the first commercial growing of trees and production of fruit. He will be remembered as the pioneer promoter of Lychees in Florida.

* * *

The lychee is an evergreen which produces clusters of round fruits that range in size from a large strawberry to a fair size lime. When ripe the fruit has shades of light red, dark red or maroon and even a tint of purple now and then. The outside skin is rough and parchment-like with small sharp points. The pulp is firm and juicy, without rag, milky white in color and very sweet in flavor, and has a distinctive fragrance. With the exception of the Longan and other close relatives, the lychee has a flavor unlike any other fruit. There is as much difference in the flavor or taste of the dried form (so-called leechee nut) and the fresh fruit, as there is between a raisin and a grape. The dried form is similar in appearance to a dried prune. The harvest season in Flor-

Late Col. Wm. R. Grove, Sr. and clusters of Brewster variety lychees.

ida is usually from June 15th to July 15th. A good portion of the fruit is shipped to areas with a large Oriental population. Some of the fruit is frozen and sold in super-markets or kept in deep freeze for home use.

The original plantings of lychee were known as the BREWSTER variety, and this is still the leading producer, however many other varieties are now available. They seldom come true from seed, so they are propagated by the air-layering method mentioned in the section on propagation. Many people do plant seeds to try their luck in obtaining new seedlings of promise. Records show that there are more varieties of lychees in the world than any other fruit, so in the years to come we can expect many more to be grown in Florida. Col. Grove introduced a later variety which he called the "Late Globe," and it is also much larger than the Brewster.

* * *

The lychee is both a fruit and ornamental tree and will reach to 40 feet in time. Average tree height however is from 25 to 30 feet. There is a large tree in Auburndale, Fla. known as the Kirkland tree which has produced as much as $900

LYCHEE FRUIT — showing clusters of ripe fruit, peel partly rmoved to show white pulp seeds (not edible) which vary in size, and foliage.

ducers. These experts say that young trees in one to five gallon cans should be planted in this manner: the planting hole should be at least three feet across and 18 inches deep, and filled with six pounds of pulveriled sheep manure, six pounds sewage sludge, and four pounds of super-phosphate, to which is added one-half bushel of well rotted compost. Let this mixture (which should be mixed thoroughly) stand for at least two weeks before planting time. For larger trees, increase size of hole, depth and plant food mixture. When you are ready to plant, be sure the hole is large enough to accommodate root system. Use a broom handle of stick to tamp down the soil. Water freely using from 5 to 10 gallons per tree. Leave a basin around the tree. It is advisable to use a mulch of wood shavings or decayed matter such as grass or leaves.

FEEDING LYCHEE TREES

Young trees are fed with a 4-8-5 formula every 60 days. For best results the nitrogen should be 40 to 50% derived from natural sources. About one-half to one pound of the 4-8-5 formula is used per feeding, and to this add one or two pounds of sewage sludge (or Milorganite) or you may use a half-bushel of well rotted cow manure. All this is added to the basin around the tree. During the Summer, give two or three good waterings for each tree every week, especially if there has been no rainfall. On established or fairly large trees, give a foliage feeding once every three months. This is optional, but worthwhile for better color and production.

in revenue in one season. In China there are trees over 100 years old and still producing heavily. The first large scale plantings in Florida were in the Bradenton-Sarasota area. Other sections have expanded very rapidly and now we have large plantings in the Ridge section, and on the East Coast from Merritt Island to Miami. There are many dooryard plantings in Pinellas and other counties, plus many small groves. It takes about 50 trees per acre when planted 40 feet apart. Some plant their groves 25 feet apart. Cost of air-layered trees range from $5.00 each on up to $50 for a large tree. Many bearing-size trees can now be purchased from $10 to $20 each. Trees that bear some fruit within three years will average about $5 to $8 each. Once you get fair size trees, you can start more by air-layering of good sized branches with a symmetrical top. Some nurseries sell small trees in large cans or tar-paper containers. The practical range of planting for the state is from Orlando southward, however some have been grown in the Sanford area. Wherever citrus will grow—lychees will grow—so say the experts. In China some have grown at the same latitude as Gainsville.

* * *

The Experimental Farm connected with the University of Miami did much with Lychees under the direction of Dr. S. John Lynch and Roy Nelson. This area is now one of the largest pro-

* * *

What is known as wind-burn causes the leaves of young trees to have the appearance of not being healthy or to be lacking in nutrients. Do not get alarmed as this is natural if no windbreak has been provided. It is best to protect young trees from both the wind and the sun for a good part of the day, especially during the time from 11 A.M. until 3 P.M. Use 1x2 or 1x3 stakes arranged in triangular fashion (and high enough) covered with burlap, for your shading of trees. Well established trees seldom need this protection. However for dooryard planting it has been found, that trees near buildings are protected from extreme cold spells.

Avocados

THE AVOCADO ranks high as a door-yard or commercial fruit in Florida, and extremely high for its health benefits. Its pulp when ripe is used in salads of many descriptions, or if beaten into a butter-like consistency it is tasty as a spread for bread or crackers. It is often mixed with mayonnaise, or with onions or tomatoes and other appetizing items.

The Avocado is rich in proteins, oil and fats, minerals and vitamins, especially vitamins A and B. Because of its bland nature and oil content, many recommend it for ulcer diets. Most of the cafeterias and restaurants offer avocados in slices or in salads, etc., during the season.

RACES OF AVOCADOS

Although many commercial avocados are in Florida, a good many come from California, Central America, Mexico and Cuba. Nearly all the avocados raised in Florida come from the West Indian, Mexican or Guatemalan races. Seedlings and crosses from these three races account for the named varieties growing in the state and elsewhere. There are perhaps hundreds of named varieties in the state, but the following have proven the most popular and practical for either home or commercial plantings: The LULA, BOOTH No. 7 and No. 8, HALL, TAYLOR, ITZAMNA, POLLOCK, TRAPP, and the WALDIN. Before describing each of these popular avocados, let's give the main characteristics of the three races mentioned.

MEXICAN race is one of the hardiest of avocados, and is recommended for the most northerly parts of the growing areas, or from Vero Beach on the East Coast and Pasco County on the West Coast. Fruit from avocados of this race range from three to 15 fifteen ounces, with a color range from green to purple, and with a high oil content. Skin is very thin, about the same as an apple. Maturity season in Florida runs from June through November.

GUATEMALAN race produces large fruit with a color range from pale green to dark purple. Skin is hard and thick on most varieties of this race. They are more cold resistant than the West Indian types, but not as much as the Mexican types. Temperatures of 23 degrees have been reported without serious damage to trees. From blossom to maturity it takes 10 to 12 months. Blooming overlaps those of West Indian race. Fruiting season varies from October to June, depending on variety.

WEST INDIAN race of Avocados usually have smooth, thin leathery skin. Fruit is usually small but of excellent flavor, however there are some of this group that do bear fairly large fruit. Blooms appear from February to April and ripe fruit within six to nine months.

VARIETIES MOST PLANTED

From Dade County where the largest commercial plantings are in Florida, a survey indicates that about two-thirds of all trees planted were of the varieties described as follows:

LULA ranks number one in most trees planted and bearing. It has a pyriform or pear-shape fruit with slightly roughened skin of green color and averages from 14 to 24 ounces in weight. The flesh or pulp has good texture and flavor with an oil content from 12 to 16 per cent. The seeds are large. Many hundreds of Lula Avocado trees are grown in Central Florida areas, some of the real old ones are very tall and strong and make ideal shade trees as well as fruit producers.

BOOTH numbers 7 and 8 rate as heavy producers of medium to large fruit that is smooth and bright green in color. Booth No. 7 has light yellow flesh. Ripening season is from December to January 15th. Booth No. 8 has light cream-colored flesh. Ripening season from November to December 15th.

HALL which is a trifle larger than the Booth varieties is gaining fast. Flesh is deep yellow and very good flavor. Skin is of dark-green color. Reports indicate consistent bearing from November through December.

TAYLOR which is of the Guatamalan race is a very good commercial and home variety which has been grown in Florida since 1914. Its fruit is also of the pyriform shape and averages from 12 to 18 ounces. The skin is rough and pebbled and of dark-green color. The flesh is very rich in flavor and of light yellow color. Oil content ranges from 13 to 17 per cent. It is said to be more cold resistant than any other commercial variety. More upright in growth than the Lula and considered a very strong tree.

ITZAMNA is another avocado of the Guatemalan race that produces fruit the size of the Taylor. Fruit ripens from March to May and takes one year from blossoms to maturity. Some other well known avocados of the Guatamalan race grown in Florida include the TAFT, LINDA, WAGNER, MAC DONALD, and EAGLE ROCK.

POLLOCK is one of the largest avocados of the West Indian race. Grown commercially for many years, however it is considered a shy-bearing variety and very susceptible to cold spells. Better suited to warmer areas of state. It is a rapid growing tree, and produces fruit that weighs from 16 to 36 ounces. Flesh is rich yellow blending with green near the skin. Matures from July to September. Suitable for dooryard tree.

TRAPP is a widely planted variety of the West Indian race. It bears pale to yellowish-green fruit which is roundish-oblate shape, and averages from 10 to 24 ounces in weight. The ripe fruit is smooth rich golden-yellow color and with a delicate nutty flavor. Season of ripe fruit is from

September to January with peak months being October and November. This avocado is excellent for shipping.

WALDIN is a popular avocado of the West Indian race, particulary in South Florida areas. One of the most vigorous and hardy in this race. Fruit is oblong, with an offset at one side of the blossom end, and averages from 12 to 24 ounces. Very rich flesh of pale yellow to greenish-yellow color. Because it is highly productive it has a tendency to overbear. Season of ripe fruit is from October 15th to January.

ABOUT GROWING AVOCADOS

Fall is considered the best time to plant avocados in Florida, however they seem to grow no matter what time they are planted if properly watered and fed. During the dry months, watering should be at least twice a week. You can purchase excellent grafted stock from nurseries or plant specialists in the area where avocados are grown. It is possible to start them from seed, however they seldom come true and it takes a much longer time for a seedling tree to bear fruit (sometimes they never bear). On the other hand a good many new avocados have been started from seeds. The seeds from mature fruit will remain viable for three to four weeks after taking from the fruit. Seeds from the West Indian races are often used to produce rootstock for budding or grafting. Some claim the other races are equally suitable, however records show preference to those of the West Indian race. Seeds are planted in a fairly deep box or container filled with good soil or compost, or well matured sawdust wetted down with a nutrient solution made from soluble plant food. When the diameter of the seedling is about 3/8 of an inch, it is ready for budding. Shield budding is preferred by most growers. Another method used in Florida is called side grafting. When the rootstock is about pencil size, the scion would be about the same thickness. For more details on budding and grafting of avocados consult your county agent or secure a copy of the book EVERGREEN ORCHARDS by Wm. H. Chandler (Pub. by Lea and Febigen, Philadelphia, Pa.).

* * *

Avocados will not thrive in low wet places, for they do not like wet feet. Good drainage is a necessity. A good mulch too is very helpful. This may be straw, grass, hulls, etc., or it may be a living mulch. Experiments in recent years indicate that a living mulch such as Bryophyllums or Kalanchoes help give a superior production. *Bryophyllum pinnatifolium* is suggested. This plant goes under such common names as Cathredal Bells, Lucky Leaf or Life plant. Every leaf or part of a leaf will sprout and form a living mulch in very short time. They also put blooms (Cathedral Bells) on tall stalks about Christmas each year. No doubt a good many of the other plants of this classification would be just as effective for a mulch. As most soils where avocados are grown are defici-

ent in humus or organic matter, it is advisable to add such materials to the planting hole when setting out new plants. You can use home-made composts, or commercial types, or peat mixed with well-rotted manures can be used. Colloidal phosphate is excellent for holding moisture in root area and makes other plant foods more effective. Commercial planters use leguminous cover crops (which are plowed under) such as Crotolaria, Velvet Beans, Pigeon Peas, Hairy Indigo and others. For home planting allow 30 feet between trees. Commercial groves space 20 x 20 or 25 x 25 feet.

FEEDING AVOCADOS

What fertilizer or plant food should I use on my avocados is of course a very debatable subject, and varies in each locality. Ordinarily the 6-6-8 formula will do in most cases. A nutritional spray is used by most growers to overcome zinc deficiency which is apt to cause dying back and yellowing of leaves. Minorel and Sesquestrene is recommended to supply many of the needed minor elements and iron. (Both have directions on package). Many dealers in the avocado areas have specially prepared formulas for all the avocado feeding schedules. For home trees, you can always boost growth with an application of soluble type plant foods, but remember you also use slow acting plant foods for long lasting results.

Most all plants have insect pests or diseases to cope with, and the avocado is no exception. It has foliage diseases that affect the trunk, roots, branches and fruit. The most common are scab, cercospora, spot or blotch, and black spot. You will find much information on treatment of the diseases and pests of the avocado in a booket issued by the U. S. Department of Agriculture (Circular No. 582) and called AVOCADO DISEASES in FLORIDA. The State Dept. of Agriculture at Tallahassee, Fla., also has bulletins on the avocado.

* * *

The shock treatment has been tried by many people to bring an avocado that has been dormant for years into bearing. For what it is worth, here are the details as reported by a lady in Bradenton, Fla. Dig holes around the tree and fill with about 20 lbs. of good Citrus fertilizer (4-6-8 will do) and every six weeks do the same thing until you have used-up a 100-lb. bag of fertilizer. At first, many of the leaves will fall, but will soon grow back. This treatment is for trees whose trunks are at least 12 inches in diameter and trees from 10 years or more in age.

* * *

Botanically the AVOCADO is called *Persea americana* and is a member of the Laurel family, which includes the cinnamon, camphor, sassafras, and sweet bay trees. Avocado is derived from Aztec word "ahuacatl." In Spanish it is called "aguacate". In Brazil it is "abacate". In early days many people in this country called them Alligator Pears.

Mangos

THE MANGO IS RATED as one of the best tropical fruits of the world, and in Florida it is considered one of the best dooryard fruit trees, and also one of commercial importance. As a dooryard tree they are grown from Pinellas County southward on the West Coast and from Vero Beach to the upper keys on the East Coast. Commercially they are grown in Manatee County, and near Palm Beach area, with larger plantings in Miami-Homestead area. The mango belongs in the *Anacardiaceae* family which includes the famous Cashew and Pistachio Nut, and the Brazilian Pepper, *Schinus terebintfolius*, (commonly called the Florida Holly or Christmas Berry tree), also the poisonous Sumac, Poison Ivy and Poison Oak. The full botanical name of the mango is *Mangifera indica*.

In Florida there is what is called the common mango whose fruit is relished by many, but is very stringy and has a very piney or turpene flavor. In comparison to the many fine hybrids, the common mango doesn't stand a chance for general acceptance. They do make large trees, and are perhaps more hardy than the average hybrid types. Mangos from India, Saigon and the Philippines have played an important part in the breeding and crossing of the many hundreds of fine mangos now offered to the public. There are actually three races of mangos, classified as INDIAN, SAIGON, and PHILIPPINE.

The first new mango of the large fibre-free type and one that slices as easily as a firm peach was obtained by planting a seed of an Indian type called the MULGOBA. From this seedling came the famous HADEN MANGO named after Capt. John J. Haden of Coconut Grove, Fla. the man who was responsible for the first of the better mangos. Even today the Haden Mango still rates very high as to size, freedom from fibre, and flavor. Some people call all the better mangos a Haden, however there are so many newer ones that are better in so many ways, that the general public should be informed. The Florida Mango Forum has helped promote the better mangos, and each year there is an exhibition, with ribbons, new introductions, plus of course the discussion of growing and marketing of the mango.

When you plant a seed from one of the Indian varieties such as the Mulgoba or their offspring, as the Haden, you never know exactly what to expect, however you may get a new mango with new qualities, or you may not get anything outstanding. But that is the chance you take with many things started from seed. From the seeds of the Haden came the very outstanding Zill mango which is among the top five rated by ex-

COMMON MANGOS

perts. The Irwin, another fine mango, came from the seed of a Lippens which was from a Haden seed.

While many of the best mangos have Mulgoba and Haden parentage, there are others such as the Sandersha (large fruit to eight inches), the Brooks and the Fascell which have other Indian mangos as their parents. The Brooks is one of the better late mangos. The Fascell is considered a late variety, but not as late as the Brooks. The Anderson mango which has the Sandersha parentage is an early ripening type that is more or less oblong in shape, and considered a good flavor but not like the top five which are as follows: The Kent, Zill, Irwin, Keitt, Palmer. This list however is controversial, but still a fair guide for gardeners.

One of the finest of dooryard (also commercial) mangos of the Saigon race is one that comes true from seed and is called the Cambodiana. It is of

Mangos

CLUSTER OF FASCELL MANGOS

HADEN MANGO.

good texture and flavor, but is much smaller than the Haden and others mentioned. The Cambodiana is of long appearance, and color is yellow-green when ripe and free from dots found on so many others. The Carabao mango of the Philippine race resembles the Cambodiana, as do many others in the same classification. The late Dr. Bruce Ledin (with the Sub-Tropical Experiment Station in Homestead) along with Dr. S. John Lynch and Margaret Mustard of the University of Miami Experimental Farm, list the following in the order of their popularity:

1. Kent	10. Fascell
2. Zill	11. Lippens
3. Irwin	12. Brooks
4. Keitt	13. Sensation
5. Palmer	14. Haden
6. Davis-Haden	15. Jacquelin
7. Eldon	16. Springfels
8. Edward	17. Carrie
9. Smith	18. Dixon

WHERE CAN YOU GROW MANGOS?

Many varieties of soils are adaptable to the various mangos listed. In the Miami-Homestead area however, the soils are mostly oolithic limestone, while the Palm Beach area which includes Lake Okeechobee have mucky soils but with good drainage provided. In the Ridge or Central sections the sandy or sandy loam soils grow many fine mangos. Pine Island and Ft. Myers on the west coast grow many fine mangos in sandy loam.

In recent years the real bad cold spells have damaged or destroyed many mango plantings in the northern boundaries along the East and West Coast and even in some of the warmer areas. So it is best to consider windbreak or other protection when planting above Ft. Myers and Palm Beach.

WHAT ABOUT PLANT FOOD REQUIREMENTS

Most trees offered to the public are grafted on suitable stock and sold in large cans or containers. When they are transplanted to the ground, you can feed them with soluble type plant foods to give them a good boost. Use from one to five gallons of nutrient solution depending on size of tree, and about every 6th week spray the foliage with minor elements (Minorel or Sesquestrene). If the soil is mucky, then it is best to hold back on the nitrogen. A 5-5-5 chemical mixture is recommended, or you may use a 4-9-3 (with nitrogen at least 25% from organic sources) which is used by many commercial growers. Fertilize new plantings once a month (during Winter every 2 months) and use half pound of 4-9-3 formula per tree, and increase to one pound by end of the year. By the end of the third year the amount should be increased to 4 to 5 lbs. per tree. For detailed information of feeding, budding, grafting and general care of mango, contact your county agent or write to the Fla. State Dept. of Agriculture, Tallahassee, Fla. for the bulletin "Mangos in Florida" by Lynch and Mustard. Another helpful item is a book published by the Florida Mango Forum and called "Mango Studies" obtainable from Edwin Menninger, Stuart, Florida.

WHAT ABOUT COLD WEATHER PROTECTION

Only a few areas are considered frost-free in Florida, so when the weather bureau informs you that the temperature is going to drop in your area, it would be wise to wrap your trees from the ground up to 10 or 20 inches (on small trees) with Sisalcraft or similar material. Some use straw and heavy paper material. On larger trees Fibre-glass is recommended. Masking tape is good for binding the edges.

Papaya

THE PAPAYA is a tropical fruit produced on a herbaceous plant that is commonly referred to as a tree. The fruit is melon-like and varies in shape from a long cucumber to a huge round or pear-shaped melon. When ripe, the fruit has shades of yellow, orange or light green, and occasionally s o m e are found with a tinge of red coloring. The flavor of the Papaya has so many variations that all you can say it that "when it is good, it is very good . . . . but when it is bad, it is horrid." In other words the range is from real sweet, fairly sweet and then insipid, or as a Negro woman once said to me when she tried one that had either been touched by cold, or was an inferior melon, "I'se don't eat anymore . . because it taste like a wet dog smells."

Control of flavor is one factor that so far no one seems to know too much about. A few factors prevail in the manner of feeding and seed selection. In spite of all the bad points, there are so many good ones, that you like many others are challenged and as a result you will begin to raise acceptable or superior fruit. As an aid to disturbances of the digestive tract, bowel disorders, gastric ulcers, gastric fermentation and gastritis, the Papaya has been termed the "Miracle fruit." This is due to the presence of an enzyme similar to Pepsin and which is called Papain. This enzyme is present in the green fruit, leaves and stems of the plant, and it is commercially collected in Cuba and other parts of the world and sold in dry or powder form. It is the basis of many of the meat tenderizers and digestive tablets on the market. Health food stores sell Papain in tablet form. Likewise such products as Papene, or Papoids depend on Papain to do the work. You can even collect your own Papain and store it in air-tight bottles. Just scratch the green fruit with a toothpick, your finger-nail, or a sharp steel blade, and the thin milky juice will flow and thicken. Even the flowers and vegetative portions of the plant will yield papain. When the juice has thickened, scrape into a glass and let it dry in the shade until it forms into a white powdery substance. Be careful not to get any of the fresh papain on the hands or skin. Workers who collect papain commercially have to wear gloves. A pin point of pure papain is often used in removing warts.

Fruit of the Papaya is served the same as the cantaloupe. The melon is cut lengthwise and sprinkled with the juice of the lemon or lime. Some leave the seeds in the halves and eat them with the pulp. Authorities say this is foolish and not advisable because only the very thin covering of the seeds contains a minute trace of Papain, and that the rest of the seed is very hot and harmful to the system.

PAPAYA JUICE

Papaya juice is a favorite drink with many people, and if it is made right and flavored with citrus juices, ginger, and perhaps a little honey . . . then it is delicious. First of all, there is really no such thing as Papaya juice, what is sold is mainly the pulp whipped into a consistency then thinned with other juices. There is so little juice in the melon itself that it would be unprofitable to make a drink of unadulterated papaya juice. Some of the so-called Papaya juices sold on the market taste like a cheap perfume, so you have to experiment a little to find the right one. If you have good ripe fruit on hand, it can be placed in a blender or Osterizer type machine and mixed with Temple orange or tangerine, grape fruit, or Calomondin slices or sections, add some good honey like Tupelo Honey or Orange Blossom Honey, a dash of ginger (optional) and there you have a superb Papaya juice drink.

* * * *

When cooking meats or roasts, just add a few four inch squares of the green fruit and your food will be so tender that it will almost fall apart. If you prefer, the meat tenderizers like Adolph's will also do the trick. In the West Indies the natives wrap meats and roasts (and fowl) with the leaves of the Papaya before baking or cooking.

When the green melon is cooked like squash it becomes a very healthful vegetable dish for the table. Remember, it has to be the green or unripe fruit.

Papaya fruit is used for making many very delicious items for home consumption, such as pie, jelly, salads, sherbert, sauce, papaya butter, conserve, chutney, pickles, cocktails, canapes, heavenly hash, and many stewed or baked dishes.

GROWING PAPAYAS

Except in a few instances, all Papayas are propagated by seed. They are sown in a seed flat, can or even the open ground. Plant bands made of felt paper or veneer are used by many growers. Put a handful of peat moss in the bottom of the plant band or can to hold the moisture, or you may use any of the rooting mediums described in this book. Use about seven or eight seeds of the male and female or unisexual type of seeds for each container and cover with one-quarter to a half inch of soil, or a layer of vermiculite. If you use the type known as bisexual (requires no male plant) then use only three or four seeds per container. Be sure and water often enough to keep the top inch of soil from becoming dry, but don't saturate. Small seedlings are subject to damping-off if regular soil is used without sterilizing. Vermiculite or Perlite is sterile and requires no treatment. Two to three weeks are required for the appearance of seedlings. Dried or fresh seeds take about same amount of time to germinate.

When the plants have reached four to six inches in height, they should be thinned out by removing the weaker seedlings. Leave about two to the can or container for bisexual seeds or four for the unisexual type. Before transplanting to the open field, the small plants should be hardened in the sun for a few days. Plants may be set out as soon as they have six or more leaves.

Some growers sow the seeds from January to March, and set out the seedlings in March or April. This offers some drawbacks to areas subject to cool weather in the Fall, and where there is no frost protection. The main reason for planting during these months is to have fruit for the tourist season. Late Summer planting has certain advantages in this respect, for the fruiting starts after the cool weather has passed. Plants set out in March or April run the risk of inferior fruit, for the cool weather plus shortened length of day checks the full development of the melons. It has been shown that a lowering or reducing of sugar content by just two to three percentage units from normal is sufficient to render the fruit unsatisfactory. Another factor to consider is the wind or hurricane damage that usually occurs when the crop is in full flesh and perhaps loaded with fruit. The setting of plants in the Fall has many advantages over the Spring plantings. They will produce a considerable quantity of fruit before the windy or hurricane season, and if no hurricane they will produce all Summer and still make a larger Winter crop. Stambaugh, a noted Papaya authority, says the month of April is best for starting the seeds, for small seedlings or plants can be protected easily during the hurricane season, and will recover if partly injured, whereas a fully loaded plant would be a total loss. Fall settings can be made any time from August to last of October. Certain varieties or strains will fruit from seed in 10 to 12 months, while others, like Solo from Hawaii (and Stambaugh strains), take from 12 to 18 months or more to bear fruit.

PAPAYA FLOWERS

The type of flowers determine whether a papaya is one of three sex forms: First—Female or Pistillate. Second — Bisexual or Hermaphrodite. Third — Male or Staminate. The flowers also determine the shape or type of fruit to some extent.

(1) FEMALE — Possesses a functional ovary, but lacks stamens. Depends upon an outside source of pollen for fertilization. (See photo). Fruit from female flowers are more or less spherical to obovoid.

(2) BISEXUAL — The bisexual or hermaphrodite flowers are divided into several classifications. Normally the bisexual types produce both fruit and pollen in the same flower. They also produce flowers that resemble the male plant, and

function as a male for the purpose of furnishing pollen to any females in the vicinity. The following are the accepted classifications:

(A) PENTANDRIA — because they possess five stamens which are fairly short and appear to alternate with the petals. Usually produces globular or slightly oblong fruit with five deep longitudinal grooves.

(B) CARPELLOID — or intermediate bisexual flowers. It is termed intermediate because of its lack of definite arrangement. The young buds are often distorted. Petals may be nearly free to their base, or fused together and with pistil as much as two-thirds of their length. Stamens vary from two to ten in number. They are carpel-like in structure. Fruit from this type of flower often assumes grotesque forms.

(C) ELONGATA — this type of flower has elongated pistils and the fruit in general is of the long cylindrical shape. There is another flower of this type that sometimes fails to develop a functional pistil, although there is a vestigial ovary lacking stigmas always present. This is known as a "barren" hermaphrodite form, and occurs only at certain seasons of the year.

(3) MALE — The male or staminate flowers produce no fruit. The pistil is present, but is reduced to a rudiment and lacks stigmas. The male flower produces only pollen and is the complement to the female or pistillate flower. The flowers of the male appear on long or pendulous stems. Usually, only two male plants are required for every 12 female plants.

TYPES OF FRUIT FROM BISEXUAL SEEDS

Back row — left to right: Female of bisexual variety; Male of bisexual variety (seldom found on same plant) ; Extremes of the bisexual variety; Fruit from Female plant. No. 5, the extreme. Cucumber shapes. Extremes from Elongata (C).

Papaya

PAPAYA VARIETIES

There are only a few recognized so-called varieties of the Papaya. The average run of plants on the market are from open pollinated plants, or in other words the pollination is left to a Sphinx Moth (resembling a humming-bird) that may be seen near plants in the early morning or at dusk. This method is sort of haphazard and not very dependable. Good strains often occur accidently, however most of the best ones come from hand-pollination and bagging of flowers. The following are a few of the named varieties that are popular in Florida, but not always obtainable without a lot of search.

The Solo is a favorite from Hawaii and on account of the small size it is a good melon for marketing and shipping. It averages about one pound, is either round or pear-shaped, and usually of good flavor. It is a bisexual type and requires no male plants, however the rule is that only a certain percentage of seeds of bisexuals remain so, and that males will appear also. The Blue Stem is another favorite and is of the bisexual Elongata type. Leaf petioles and fruit pedicels are from bluish lavender to purple in color. Fruit from four to eight pounds, long, oblong or tapering at the stem end. Rind is rough and dark green with light yellowing at maturity.

The Stambaugh Blue Solo represents many years of selection and breeding by Scott U. Stambaugh a recognized authority of Miami. It is one of the most ideal and true melons so far, and is said to be more uniform in size and flavor.

The Betty variety is classed as the semi-dwarf type. Produces basal fruits within 18 to 24 inches of the ground. Starts flowering two to three months from seed. Fruits are rounded-oblong and range from two to three pounds in weight. Fairly thick flesh and of dessert quality. The late Wm. L. Ems of St. Petersburg, Florida, kept this strain going for many years.

The Fairchild variety is recommended for fine fruit and is perhaps more cold resistant than most varieties. Fruits are borne fairly low on the stem and on short pedicels. Flesh is thick and firm. Fruit usually ripens in five months after hand pollinating.

Many new names have appeared in market or state bulletins, and some are no doubt good, but only trial and experience will determine this.

PAPAYA NOTES

Papayas will not stand wet feet. Four hours in standing water usually means their doom. So your first consideration is high and dry places, or where drainage can be provided. It is advisable to make beds that are from 12 to 18 inches higher than regular soil level. Plant your seedlings in beds eight to 10 feet each way. Mulch all plants to help retain moisture and to keep down root-knot. Some use shavings, leaves, straw or mixtures. Plant close to buildings for protection, or provide windbreak plants like the Cajeputs, Java Plum, Viburnums, Pigeon Peas, and others that hug the ground or have fairly dense foliage.

* * *

Most any good or well made compost can be used for fertilization, however Papayas require twice as much plant food as most other plants and any composted material should be supplemented by using a 4-10-12 formula (Stambaugh) or fish scraps, chicken manure, plus colloidal phosphate. Further information on Papayas may be obtained from your county agent or write to Florida State Dept. of Agriculture, Tallahassee, Florida, for the bulletin "Papaya Culture in Florida," or Bulletin No. 113 from the Agriculture Extension Service, Gainesville, Florida. A very elaborate bulletin (Bulletin No. 87) may be obtained from the Hawaii Agriculture Experiment Station, University of Hawaii, in Honolulu, T. H.

PAPAYA (Unisexual) This type requires no male plants, as both types of flowers are produced on same plant. Betty variety is similar.

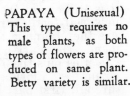

Male Blossoms

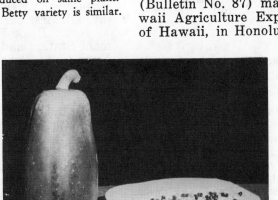

Standard Bisexual Melon

Female Blossom

Grapes for Florida

WHEN I WAS A BOY, it was a great experience to pull Scuppernong grapes off the huge wooden arbors on the farms of my relatives all over the North and Northwest Florida. Among the natives, the word "Scuppernong" was synonymous with grapes, and the other kinds were shipped in. I didn't find out until many years later that Scuppernongs was only a variety of a group known as Muscadines which have been growing from Virginia southward ever since the days of Sir Walter Raleigh. Even today there are scores of people who call all Muscadine grapes either a white, bronze or black Scuppernong. Several years ago my wife and I visited the 60 acre vineyard of the late Dr. Chas. Demko in Altoona, Fla. on highway Fla. 19 near Leesburg, where we tasted a dozen or more varieties of Muscadines before sampling the familiar Scuppernong variety. When it came to sweetness, lack of after taste and thinner skin, they did not compare with the majority. However, they are still very hardy and dependable producers.

Simple trellis for home growing
of bunch grapes.

The various named Muscadines on the market were developed from two botanical species. *Vitis rotundifolia* (called Bullace grapes by natives) and *Vitis munsoniana* (bird grapes). The last named is a native of Florida and many are found in the woods and along roads and creeks. Nearly all the Muscadines have thick hulls, but some of newer hybrids are much thinner than older varieties such as the Scuppernong and the Flowers. There is also quite a variety of colors in the highly flavored juices. Of those we tried, I would place the one named Topsail at the head of the list for fresh fruit or table use. It is of light bronze color, — large fruit, and very sweet — and a thinner skin.

Lucida was second on our list, being very sweet, slightly smaller and darker in color.

Among the darker-colored varieties the Dulcet was third in our choice, and it is a reddish-purple grape that is very sweet and with thin skin. Fruit remains on vine until they shrivel. One of the best eating varieties. Hunt rates very high with its large black grapes with medium thin skin and excellent flavor. Grows in bunches. Thomas is one of the old-time reddish-purple muscadines with a pleasing flavor. Of course there are several other hybrids that rate high, but this is a good starter list. Suggest you write for Dr. Demko's bulletin called "Growing Grapes in Florida". It is obtainable from your county agent or from State Dept. of Agriculture in Tallahassee, Fla.

We continued our Muscadine Exposition by visiting another well known grape man connected with the Georgia Experiment Station at Experiment, Ga., Mr. B. O. Fry who has done considerable grape growing and hybridizing. He told me that their Higgins variety had proven one of the top producers of the bronze-colored Muscadines. Today it is still one of the tops for Fla. and Georgia. Two new self-fertile bronze Muscadines now available are the Magnolia and Carlos. Mr. Fry also recommends the dark-colored Hunt, Dulcet and Creek varieties plus the Topsail, Yuga and Higgins. Fruit ripens in Florida from the middle of August through first part of September.

Note: B. O. Fry has retired from the Experiment Station and is now connected with the ISON Nursery at Brooks, Ga. (They will send you a catalog.)

* * *

A pollinating type is necessary in all Muscadine plantings regardless of size. At leat one pollinator type is required for every nine female producing male vines. A number of self-fertile muscadines have replaced non-producing male vines. and these help to increase the yield. Four are highly recommended by the Georgia Experiment Station and Dr. Demko. They are the dark-fruited Burgaw and Tar-heel, the bronze-colored Willard and Wallace varieties. Tarheel is the most vigorous and produces the most blossoms, but its fruit is small and has low acid content. Burgaw has better flavor and is slightly larger in size.

Grapes for Florida

PLANTING MUSCADINES

Grapes require well drained soil that is fertile. If you plant only a few vines, then you can build up poor or medium soils with organic materials, composts, humus and manures. Composts with manures, plus about five pounds of colloidal phosphate and five pounds of Hybro-tite (ground potash rock) should be incorporated in four or five foot square areas to a minimum depth of 18 inches. A good soaking with a soluble plant food also helps to start off new vines.

The planting season in Florida is usually from late November to February. In South Georgia it is from late December through March. Same applies to Alabama, Mississippi and Louisiana.

When planting in rows, the vines should be set 20 feet apart, and it is best to set a post to a depth of three feet, with five feet extending up from the soil level. By placing the post close to the newly set vine, it is easy to train it and provide good support.

Only one wire is required from one post to the other, and it may be No. 10 smooth galvanized wire. The use of the second wire midway between top and the ground is optional.

The use of only one wire requires less time in harvesting and pruning, makes cultivation much easier, and is more economical in large plantings. Most of the crop is produced on the arms along the top-wire anyway, so there is really no necessity of the second or third wire system. The end posts should be braced in order to hold the heavy vines when in fruit. Each row that you plant should have at least 10 to 12 feet spacing in between. This allows for cultivation, and for growing of cover crops which can be turned over to enrich the soil. You may grow strawberries, vegetables, or other subsidiary crops in between rows.

PLANT FOOD REQUIREMENTS

One half pound of an 8-8-8 (complete fertilizer) is used for each vine the first growing season. Scatter within a two-foot circle, but out at least four inches from the trunk. Apply from March 1 to 15th in middle South areas and 30 days earlier in Florida areas. Ninety days later, side-dress with quarter of a pound of nitrate of soda per vine applied in same manner as fertilizer. The second year the amounts are doubled. The third and succeeding years the complete fertilizer and nitrate applications will vary from two to three pounds, and should be broadcast along the row before vine growth starts in the Spring.

The use of Minorel or Sesquestrene on foliage every second month from time of planting, or 60 days after each complete fertilizer application, will help the flavor, color and final yield.

TRAINING AND PRUNING

To establish the framework of the vine, it is necessary to prune during the Summer, and also during the dormant season for the first two or three years. Summer pruning consists of removal of all canes not needed to form the main trunk, and of pinching back the lateral growth on the trellis arms to three or four joints. This operation should be repeated during the growing season. One effective method of training is to tie a string to a stub of a cane near the base of the main stem, and to the trellis wire, permitting the main stem to attach its tendrils to the string and to climb it to the trellis wire.

Example of single wire
trellis for Muscadines.

Dormant season pruning requires cutting back all lateral shoots on the arms to three or four buds and removal of side growth on the trunk. If you do not prune during the Summer, you will have to remove much more growth during the dormant season that should have been forced into forming the framework.

When the framework has been established, annual dormant pruning is simple but important job that results in better production of fruit. The short-spur method is recommended for this annual pruning. This consists of cutting back all the current season's growth to spurs of two to four inches long that have three to five buds. Any side growths from the trunk and tendrils that may girdle the arms are cut off.

Pruning at the proper time to avoid "bleeding" of the sap at the cut ends is very important. Usually the best time is from four to six weeks after the first killing frost in November. In Florida, where there is seldom any frost at this time, pruning should not be later than December. Eight years of testing at the Georgia Experiment Station showed that vines pruned the latter part of February maintained their vigor and produced yields equal to vines pruned in November. So al-

Grapes for Florida

though experts recommended that the pruning operation be completed during the early part of the dormant season, they say that if anything should prevent that, then the pruning should be delayed until just before growth begins in the Spring. The light colored Topsail should not be pruned as heavily as other muscadines.

GRAPE SOURCES

Aubrey Owens Nursery
Gay, Ga. 30218

Davis J. Midulla Nursery
4302 Woodmere Road
Tampa, Fla. 33606

Ison Nursery
Brooks, Ga. 30205

BUNCH GRAPES FOR FLORIDA GARDENS

A visit with L. H. Stover of the Watermelon and Grape Laboratory (Division of Univ. of Fla.) at Leesburg, Fla., revealed much about bunch grapes in Florida. Mr. Stover says that over 400 varieties have been tried here in the last 35 or 40 years, but practically all have failed because of a condition known as de-generation, die-back or decline. Some varieties do well for a number of years, then start a gradual decline. Finally, after many years of crossing and testing, the Lake Emerald was obtained by crossing a native white-fruited grape known as the Pixiola (*Vitis simsponi*) with the cultivated yellow-fruited Golden Muscat variety. The cross was made in 1944 and since has proven worthy of growing as a home grape. Flowering occurs from late March to April 15th. Maturity is usually from July to early August. Eighteen-month old vines bore 15 to 20 pounds of marketable fruit per vine in 1953. Excellent reports have been received from Homestead to North and Northwest parts of Florida, and all state heavy yields of fruit. The Lake Emerald is one of the best for the home garden or arbor planting. Berries grown in diffused sunlight develop a golden color when ripe. They are slightly smaller than most Concord type grapes found on the market, but are far sweeter than most shipped in grapes. They make excellent juice that is sweet and aromatic, but light in color.

In planting the Lake Emerald grape, sunlit areas away from competition with trees and shrubs are recommended. The one-wire system described for the muscadines can be used, or the usual home-type arbor is ideal. Mr. Stover recommends that rows be laid out running east and west, using the standard three-wire Kniffin trellis (top wire near top of post, bottom wire three feet from

ground, and second wire between the top and bottom). Growing vines should be thrown over the south side of the trellis to aid in shading.

Dormant pruning in Central Florida should be done in January. Mature plants should be pruned to a bearing frame-work of three to four canes of new wood with a total of 30 to 40 buds. Fruiting canes on the Lake Emerald can usually be pruned shorter than most other bunch grapes grown in the state.

Clean cultivation the entire years is recommended. However in established vineyards, no cultivation is needed from fruit harvest to December. A cover crop such as Hairy Indigo is very helpful. It is disked or plowed for cleaning up late in Fall.

Spraying is seldom required with muscadine grapes, but with bunch grapes in Florida there should be one in the Spring when the buds are about two inches long, and every 10 days to two weeks thereafter until the berries have attained maximum size. Recommended fungicidal spray is 1½ lbs. of Zineb to 100 gallons of water. Discontinue any spraying at least five weeks before harvest of fruit. For insect control use one pound of Lindane per 100 gallons of water. For complete details on the Lake Emerald Grape write for bulletin by L. H. Stover, at Watermelon and Grape Laboratory, Leesburg, Fla., Circular S-68.

* * *

Several new grapes have been released by the Experiment Station in the last few years. The Blue Lake which is dark colored bunch grape with a very spicy flavor. More recently is another dark grape (purple grape) called the Norris which may be planted in all Fla. above Lake Okeechobee. This one produces heavy clusters and very fine flavor. Requires a pollinator variety nearby. Lake Emerald or Blue Lake is recommended for this purpose. One of the best of the new bunch grapes for Fla. is the STOVER. It is a golden-fruited, longlived, variety with improved dessert and holding qualities that is ideal for a table grape for Fla. Both the NORRIS and the STOVER do best when grafted on Dogridge or Lake Emerald stock. Blue Lake and Norris will also grow on their own stock. Further details may be obtained from Agricultural Exp. Station Univ. of Fla., Gainesville, Fla. Blue Lake . . . Circular S-120 . . . Stover S-195 . . . Norris S-177.

* * *

If you are interested in making juice, jams, jellies, marmalades, conserves, grape butter, canned grapes, spiced grapes, etc., write for bulletin called "Processing Mascadine Grapes" (Bulletin No. 17) to the Georgia Experiment Station, Experiment, Ga. Also Press Bulletin No. 603 on the Muscadine Vineyard by B. O. Fry is very helpful.

Hydroponic Gardening

SINCE REX McDILL, a manufacturer of soluble plant foods in Tampa, Florida has introduced his method of growing tomatoes, and numerous o t h e r vegetables, flowers, bulbs, and plants of all kinds in ordinary untreated shavings and sawdust, it has spread like wild-fire all over the country. The author in his magazine articles and Radio-Garden broadcasts helped start this practical and profitable method back in 1955. First it was called the Bean-Hamper Method for growing tomatoes, but later it was found that you could use large cans, such as five gallon types (used for so many things) and produce even better results with less effort and cost. Because the familiar wood hampers used for shipping beans, and other vegetables are easily obtained from your local stores or markets, you may want to try them first. However, it is sometimes just as easy to obtain five gallon egg cans (or powdered milk cans) from bakeries or nurseries.

WHY USE THE WOOD-SHAVINGS METHOD?

First of all the flavor of tomatoes grown in the shavings-method is far superior to the average run grown in soil. Second, the size and quantity is superior to most plantings in soil. Third, it makes it possible to grow things where space is a problem. However, where you have plenty of space, this method is very profitable for commercial production. Fourth, there is no cultivation problem, such as weeding, hoeing, etc. Fifth, you can grow by this method plants that will not produce in soil. For instance, some have grown honey-dew melons and many types of bulbs that have never been successful in Florida soils and climate. Sixth, very little equipment is needed, and the cost in comparison to results is very small. Seventh, older people, or those who are crippled, may enjoy growing flowers, vegetables, etc.

WHAT PLANTS CAN I GROW?

Because the tomato is a universal favorite and used by almost every family in this country, the first experiments were confined to this vegetable alone. Even today, you will see thousands of Bean-Hampers, bushel baskets, or cans lined up in rows or in singles or groups growing luscious tomatoes on vines that reach as high as 10 or even 12 feet. I have seen as many as 900 hampers in less than an acre of plot growing in Tampa, Fla. Reports indicate that even two or three times that many have been grown and proven the worth of this method. With the exception of a few low-growing varieties, all tomatoes grown by this method reach from two to five times the height as when grown in soil. You may grow any variety from the small pear-shaped tomatoes to the large Ponderosa or Beefsteak type. In Florida the varieties that have been grown successfully include the Homestead, Manalucie, Rutgers, Marglobe, Ponderosa (Beefsteak) and the Jefferson which is a low-growing type. Many others such as the Peron (from Chile), Kokomo, Grothen's Globe, Oxheart, Pan America have produced excellent results. For commercial crops the Manalucie and the Homestead are recommended.

Many other edibles besides tomatoes may be grown in wood-shavings. For instance you may grow strawberries such as the Florida No. 90 (best locally) or the Missionary, Klondyke or others. Bushel baskets filled with shavings are best suited for growing of strawberries, however you may use other types of containers. Carrots, beets, turnips, and root crops do well by this method. Sweet potatoes grown in large containers like barrels, or half-barrels, large kegs, etc., are "out of this

Tomato Plants — Growing in Bean Hampers

Hydroponic Gardening

world" when it comes to flavor, size and production. Pineapples, papayas, honey-dew melons and a host of other edibles with that superior flavor are among the long list of plants grown by the Nutri-Sol Wood Shavings Hydroponic Method.

You may grow all kinds of flowers from seeds, bulbs, tuberous roots, or cuttings and with better color and quantity. Many have grown the Unwin types of Dahlia (from seed), Gerberas, Gloriosa or Climbing Lilies, Passion Flower vines, Zinnias, Marigolds, Petunias, Easter Lilies, Daylilies, Roses. In fact the list includes just about everything that will grow in soil, and some that don't thrive under ordinary conditions.

WOOD SHAVINGS OR SAWDUST

For the largest majority of plants, wood shavings are recommended over sawdust. Sawdust has a tendency to pack and prevent good aeration to the roots, however it may be used for larger type plants such as Papayas, Roses, or any plant that may become top-heavy. Most any kind of wood

shavings or sawdust may be used, such as pine, cypress, maple, redwood or oak. Old or new shavings or sawdust may be used. It is best however to use a new batch the second year. In other words, do not use the same shavings or sawdust or even the same hamper or wooden container after the first year. On specially built forms made out of cypress or redwood use an asphalt paint or sterilize after first year's use. It is also best to use new cans the second year.

GROWING TOMATOES IN BEAN HAMPERS

You can purchase any number of bean hampers for 25 cents each or less from your grocery store, market, or super-market. Fill each to the top with wood shavings. Wet down shavings with a nutrient solution of "Nutri-Sol," (one teaspoonful of Nutri-sol to each gallon of water is nutrient solution) and let them pack for two days. Be sure and keep container well filled. Next step is to secure tomato plants that have been grown in ster-

Tomatoes and vegetables growing in Bean Hampers and boxes filled with wood shavings.

ile soil or spaghnum moss. You may prefer to grow your own plants, if so let them reach a height of six inches before transplanting to bean hampers.

You will need adequate supports for the vines. There are many ways of doing this, such as wiring fishing canes (see photo) to the side of hampers, building a trellis alongside, or placing hampers near a tree or building which can provide support.

After the shavings have been thoroughly soaked, punch a hole deep enough to insert the tomato plants so that first leaves will rest on top. Pack shavings around plant. Use only one plant per hamper. Keep all hampers or containers in full sunshine all of the time. Do not cut off suckers as they will make your third and fourth crop six to eight months after planting.

NUTRIENT SOLUTION

The nutrient solution must be applied once a day, and every day. It is made as stated by using one teaspoonful of "Nutri-Sol" soluble plant food to each gallon of water used. One-half cupful per day is used on each plant for the first three weeks. By this time your plants should be about two feet high. After the three weeks it will take a quart of solution per plant. For each foot of increase in height add another half pint of solution. Add an additional gallon of water per plant each day, if no rain has occurred, a plant six feet high will evaporate six quarts of water a day, in hot and dry weather. Should the plants wilt, just add water and they will come back strong and healthy in 15 minutes. Add some nutrient solution.

* * *

Tomatoes require such large doses of minor elements, that it is not practical to feed them with the regular nutrient solution feedings, therefore it is best to spray or drench the plants once a week with "Minorel" solution (this requires only one teaspoonful to 10 gallons of water.) Minorel spraying means sturdier vines and almost doubles the fruit production.

THE CAN-GROW METHOD

A newer and perhaps better variation of wood-shavings Hydroponics is known as the "Can-Gro" method (also by Nutri-sol) and instead of using bean hampers or wooden containers, lard or egg cans are used to hold the shavings or sawdust. This method retains the nutrient solution and prevents waste of plant food and water. The feeding schedule therefore varies somewhat.

An egg (or lard) can is about nine inches in diameter and 13 inches high. To prepare the can, a series of holes (¼ to ½ inch in diameter) are cut. They are spaced two inches apart and should be about 6½ inches from bottom (or half-way

from bottom to top). With this line of holes around the can the following is provided: First, a means of storing nutrient solution to feed the lower roots and by capillary attraction of the shavings, to provide an aerated moist medium around the root crown of the plant. Second, supplies a means of utilizing without waste only the plant food and water that is used by the plant.

Fill the prepared can with shavings up to the rim of top, and wet them down with the nutrient solution. Plant same as described for Bean Hamper Method. After planting, sprinkle a teaspoonful of dry "Nutri-Sol" around the top of the shavings and water in until the lower half of can is filled with solution. Wet shavings daily and keep them moist at all times. Keep all cans in full sun.

FEEDING SCHEDULE:

Keep plant fed by using a teaspoonful to each three gallons of water used. For example, when the plant is small it will not evaporate or use too much solution, but when it is large (and they do reach 12 to 15 ft.) it may be necessary to water as much as a gallon a day. In the latter case you will need as much as a teaspoonful of "Nutri-Sol" every third day. Sprinkle the dry plant food on top of the shavings, it will dissolve with the regular waterings. Don't overflow the can at the holes for the purpose of washing in the fertilizer. What doesn't dissolve the first watering will do so on the subsequent watering.

Drench or spray plants once a week with "Minorel" solution, same as for Bean Hamper culture.

Be sure and provide supports for tomatoes.

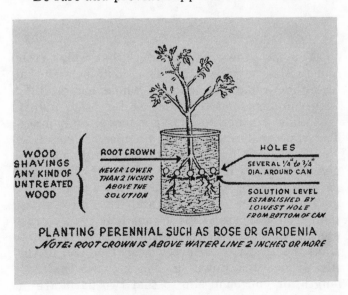

Wood Shavings Hydroponics.

Hydroponic Gardening

GROWING ROSES

Trim back roses to about root crown. The root crown is the part of the plant located between a point two inches below where the root joins the main stem of the plant. In this method of growing plants in cans and shavings, the root crown of any plant should not have any portion of it below the holes of the can.

If the rose bush has long roots, clip them off to about 10" long. Soak your shavings in "Nutri-Sol" nutrient solution, then make a layer of wet shavings about three inches deep in the can, and then hold the rose bush in can and fill in shavings up to the top rim. Remember that the point of the bush where the roots join the stem must be at least two inches above the holes in the side of the can. Water and feed same as for tomato culture.

ABOUT STRAWBERRIESS — OTHER PLANTS

Bushel baskets are ideal for strawberries. Use four plants per basket evenly spaced, but allow a few inches between rim of basket and plants. Most any variety of strawberry will grow, but for Florida use the Fla. No. 90, Tioga or Sequoia.

Bushel baskets are ideal for peppers or egg plants, lettuce, turnips, and other vegetables or flowers. For bulbs or tuberous roots you use either the baskets, the hampers or the cans. Feeding schedule, same as for tomatoes. Use method outlined for hampers and baskets, or the one outlined for can growing.

* * *

You can grow sweet potatoes that weigh from one to four pounds each. The containers should be either a hamper, half or whole barrel filled with shavings and fed same as for other plants. Use about six potato slips per barrel or hamper. The vines will run over the hamper or barrel, so you must provide runways down from top of hamper. Potatoes will cause the hamper to bulge. To get potato slips, you can either plant a good sweet potato and let it sprout and run into vines, then cut in several slips a foot long, or you can use slips that are advertised in most farm magazines the first part of every year. One end of the slip is inserted down in shavings for half its length, or you bend slip so that two parts are of equal length and push from center down into shavings.

SPRAYING FOR INSECTS

Spray most vegetables (especially tomatoes) every 10 days, or you use a good dust such as "Ortho" Vegetable Dust. Roses require dusts or sprays to keep down black spot, mildew and other pests. Consult your local garden supply houses for suitable sprays and dusts. Those that are highly poisonous should be avoided for edibles. It is dangerous to use Parathion and even Malathion unless you know how or have the proper equipment.

* * *

One final word about growing plants in wood shavings and sawdust. The method offers much for experimentation, however it has proven very worthy for such items as covered in this article. You may wonder if any other nutrient solution can be used other than "Nutri-sol", and the answer is yes, but seldom with the same results. The formulas of Nutrisol and Minorel have been worked out to give the utmost by these methods and for lawns and soils. For further details contact the "Nutrisol Chemical Co.," Box 15124, Tampa, Fla.

PAPAYA PLANT — Started from seeds sown in hamper.

Garden Calendar

Florida Planting Guide — January

ALTHOUGH THIS MONTH is considered the beginning of the New Year as far as the calendar is concerned, it is more or less the dormant season for hundreds of plants in Florida, and usually the dormant season for the gardener as far as manual labor is concerned. One thing however is evident, and that is the spectacular display of Azalea and Camellia Japonica blossoms in many of our famous gardens, parks, estates, highways and thousands of home gardens. Many cities feature Camellia and Azalea shows during January and February.

* * *

For many years the Azaleas and Camellias were placed in the group known as extreme acid loving plants, which also included Gardenias, Hydrangeas, Magnolia, Red Bud, Cajeput (Punk or Melaleuca) and many others whose natural habitat was the swamps and low areas, but in recent years certain groups of recognized authorities claim that all these plants grow equally well without the extra acidity being added to plant foods or fertilizers. They do however recognize the need for mulch and materials to retain sufficient moisture. The author has seen Azaleas grown with soluble type plant foods that equalled any grown otherwise, but it may be due to factors undetermined. Many specialists recommend the use of old sawdust, pine needles, oak leaves, straw, hulls, seed pods like those of the Mother Tongue (*Albizzia lebbek*) as mulch material. Peat is used by some, but it has a tendency to dry out quickly when used on top of soil. Peat is excellent when mixed with the soil.

* * *

AZALEAS require about twice the amount of water when they are in bloom. Instead of watering from the top, use a slow trickle from your hose or soaker around the base of the plants. Certain water sources may have too much lime, so if in doubt have your water tested.

* * *

At this time of the year, many nurseries and plant sources have plants in containers that are in bloom, thereby giving you a chance to select types and colors for your purpose.

* * *

AZALEAS are generally used for either mass planting or hedges, so in planning your garden or landscape designs, be sure and consult your nurseryman or catalog for varieties that are tall growers, medium or midget types and those suited for your location. Most azaleas are considered as sun lovers, however certain varieties do better in filtered sunlight. Plant where they can get at least half the day in the sun.

Nearly all brands of fertilizers and plant foods feature Special Azalea and Camellia formulas which may be used on any of the extreme acid loving plants. Do not use fertilizer when plants are in bloom.

* * *

Don't forget that Azaleas have a shallow root system, therefore it is not advisable to use a garden hoe around the plants. All weeds should be pulled up. A good mulch will keep the weeds to a minimum.

* * *

CAMELLIAS of the Japonica type do not like full sun, in fact they like considerable shade. Filtered sunlight caused by tall trees or shrubs are generally suitable. They also require plenty of moisture and good drainage. The Sasanqua Camellia which starts blooming as early as September and October and often lasts as long as January is a sun-loving type and often used to front the Japonica types if conditions allow sun and shade for their requirements.

* * *

If ROSES have a dormant season in Florida, this is usually the month. Many experts also claim this is the best month to plant Roses in most all areas.

* * *

ARBOR DAY is generally the third Friday in January, so why not observe it by planting some useful trees.

* * *

This is a good time to obtain bare-rooted, or balled and burlapped plants suitable for your area. Contact nearby plant sources.

* * *

SHIRLEY POPPIES are one of the easiest flowers to grow, and one of the most prolific bloomers. Although they do not require any special soil, they do better in fine pulverized types. They are seldom bothered with pests, but occasionally the tender leaves are attacked by aphis. Non-poisonous "Red Arrow Spray" will take care of this situation. Shirley Poppies come in single, semi-double or double flower types and are available in a variety of colors and patterns. The double variety resemble the flowers of the Tuberous Rooted Begonias, and do much better in Florida.

Shirley Poppies are excellent for cut flowers. It is best to cut the blossoms early in the morning, and dip about an inch of the stem in boiling water, or sear the stems.

Florida Planting Guide — January

In planting Shirley Poppies, you may sow the seeds where you want them to grow, or you may sow the seeds in a flat with a half and half mixture of builders sand and Terra-Lite (Vermiculite) and transplant the seedlings later.

One of the most useful controls for garden crops is the old reliable Bordeaux Mixture (Copper 12.5 per cent and Zinc Sulphate 10%). It is useful for spraying tomatoes for leaf spots, downy mildew, black-rot, early or late blight, and Anthracnose. Also very effective on roses, azaleas, zinnias and other flowers. Prior to bloom opening, you may spray the mixture on Mango trees. Follow up every two weeks for four successive times if weather is rainy or misty. Use a good sticker with the Bordeaux spray. Use a fine spray to keep the mixture from running.

* * *

If you are bothered with too much "SPANISH MOSS" on your Pecans, or other trees, by spraying with one or more applications of standard Bordeaux Mixture the moss will soon dry out and blow away with the wind.

* * *

Feed your Mangos this month with a 3-8-8 formula. Best time to fertilize is when the bloom buds begin to swell. Use one pound of fertilizer to each of tree trunk diameter. Circle spread to the outer reach of branches.

JANUARY AND FEBRUARY VEGETABLES

Beans	Onion Seed
Beets	Onion Sets
Brussel Sprouts	Parsley
Cabbage	Parsnip
Cantaloupe	Peas (English)
Carrot	Pepper
Cauliflower	Potatoes
Collards	Radish
Corn (Sweet)	Romaine
Cucumber	Rutabaga
Eggplant	Spinach
Endive	Squash
Kale	Swiss Chard
Kohlrabi	Tomato
Leek	Turnip
Lettuce	Watermelon
Mustard	

GRASSES AND FIELD CROP SEEDS

Alfalfa	Oats
Clover (Crimson)	Rape
Bahia Grass	Rye

JANUARY AND FEBRUARY FLOWERS

Ageratum	Marigold
Alyssum	Mignonette
Amaranthus	Myosotis (Forget Me Nots)
Arctotis (Blue-eyed African Daisy)	Nasturtium
Aster	Nemesia
Aubrietia (Rock Cress)	Nemophila (Baby Blue Eyes)
Bachelor Button (Gomphrena)	Gilia
Balsam (Impatiens)	Godetia
Browallia	Gypsophila (Baby's Breath)
Calendula	
Calliopsis	Helichrysum (Strawflower)
Campanula	Nigella
Candytuft	Pansy
Carnation	Petunia
Castor Bean	Phlox
Celosia (Cockscomb)	Poppy
Centaurea (Cornflower)	Pyrethrum (Painted Daisies)
Chrysanthemum	Salpiglossis
Clarkia	Salvia
Coreopsis	Scabiosa
Cosmos	Schizanthus
Cynoglossom (Chi. Forget Me Not)	Shasta Daisy
Cypress Vine	Snapdragon
Dahlia	Statice
Delphinium (Per. Larkspur)	Stocks
Dianthus (Pinks)	Sultana (Impatiens Sult.)
Didiscus (Blue Lace Flower)	Sweet Peas
Eschscholtzia (Calif. Poppy)	Sweet William
Gaillardia (Blanket Flower)	Thunbergia alata
Gerbera	Verbena
Hollyhock	Vinca (Periwinkle)
Kochia (Summer Cypress)	FLOWERING VINES:
Lantana	Cypress Vine
Larkspur	Moon Vine
Linaria	Morning Glories or Ipomoeas,
Lobelia	Coral Vine (Antigonon)
Lupin	Thunbergia (Black-eyed Susan Vine)
Mallows	Thunbergia fragrans
	Quisqualis (Rangoon-Creeper)

Florida Planting Guide — February

This is the time of the year that AZALEAS put out their colorful display in Florida. It is also the time when a condition known as petal blight becomes evident. This is a fungus that attacks the flowers as they begin to open, and is detected by small clear watery spots on newly opened flowers which soon wither and drop. Ask your dealer for a fungicide like Phygon or others that will correct petal blight. You might also examine the underside of leaves for Spider Mite a minute pest that sucks the juice from plants and discolors the foliage, and usually spins a slight web. Spider Mites may be whitish, reddish or greenish in color. Your dealer can supply controls like Dimite, Ridmite or others equally effective.

* * *

Remember that AZALEAS like lime-free soil.

* * *

Now is the time to plant the following bulbs or tuberous rooted plants: Dahlias (Central and North Florida), Amaryllis, Tuberous Begonias, Pink and Yellow Callas, Gladiolus, Tuberoses, and even certain Tulips in North and Central areas. Caladiums, Gloriosa or Climbing lilies, Gloxinias, Freesias, Ranunculus, Cannas, Crinums.

* * *

This is a good time to air layer plants, also for budding, inarching, grafting, and the rooting of cuttings, especially hard-wood shrubs and evergreens.

* * *

Plant Irish Potatoes now and next month. Red Pontiac certified seed potatoes are recommended. Plant at the rate of 15 lbs for each 100 feet of row. New potatoes develop in about 75 days.

* * *

Poinsettias are about through blooming during February and March, so it is advisable to cut them back partially now, and about three times in all between now and August 20th. Remember never cut them back all at once. Pinching of growing shoots or buds now and then will produce more branches and better flower bracts next season. Once every six to eight weeks, give them a good drenching of a soluble plant food like Nutrisol, Hygro, Hyponex or Cypress Gardens. Hand pick any worms that appear.

* * *

Now is a good time to feed DAYLILIES. Sidedress with any good garden fertilizer or give a good soaking with a soluble plant food. For extra color of foliage and flowers spray with MINOREL or SESQUESTRENE (Iron Chelate). Added note: Minorel or Sesquestrene is very effective on Azaleas, Camellias, Hibiscus, Ixora, Hydrangeas, Citrus and a host of other plants.

* * *

AMARANTHUS is a name for a group of plants that produce spectacular and brilliant color in their foliage. They are very useful for color during the hot summer months when there is usually a scarcity of brilliant color. Plant the seeds now where they are to grow or if you are careful you may transplant seedlings. The most spectacular Amaranthus is one called MOLTEN FIRE whose foliage is more spectacular than the Poinsettia, and is often called the Summer Poinsettia. JOSEPH COAT (Tricolor splendens) is a richly variegated red, yellow and green and very effective. Still another newer variety that is outstanding is one called DESERT SUNRAY or Baileya Multi-Radiata. Reaches a foot in height, while the other two reach about three feet. You don't always find the various Amaranthus in general runs of seed-packets so you must get them from seed specialists like the Geo. W. Park Seed Co., 308 Cokesberry Road, Greenwood, S.C. 29647 . . . Hastings Seed Co., Atlanta, Ga. . . . World Seed Service (Catalog 50c), Box 1058G, Redwood City, Cal. 94064.

* * *

Divide Chryanthemums at this time. Also Stokesia (Stokes Aster), Shasta Daisies, and Phlox.

* * *

Do most of your spring pruning the latter part of month. Cut back all tall and leggy plants, hedges, etc., to induce low-branched growth. Hibiscus needs pruning at this time to assume compact shape and prolific blooming. Be sure and use sharp pruning shears, and it is a good idea to coat all cuts on wood of ½ inch or more. Your dealer has pruning paint for the purpose.

* * *

85

Florida Planting Guide — February

FLAME VINE — Glory of January and February. Brilliant orange honeysuckle-like flowers. Climbs trees, fences & trellis.

This is an excellent time to move large trees and shrubs. They should be balled and burlapped or a large amount of compact soil should encircle each plant, and have sufficient depth so that it will not fall apart easily.

* * *

Usually during the latter part of February there is much evidence of green in our lawns and also in the weeds that come up in the Spring. Start pulling weeds as they appear then give your grass a good soaking with a soluble plant food like Nutrisol, etc., and another in about two weeks. You may use any good lawn fertilizer with plenty of organics, or use manure applications. Soluble plant foods are easy to apply with the aid of one of the many types of guns that attach to your garden hose. For that extra green color give an application of Minorel or Sequestrene once or twice in a two months period.

* * *

Camellias should also be fertilized now, and you have many good special purpose formulas available at your garden supply houses. White fly and aphids may appear after the danger of frost has gone. Spray with Florida Volck or suitable oil emulsion, and do this when the temperature is between 45 and 90 degrees.

* * *

One of the old-time garden favorites that is staging a come-back is the CANNA or some say Canna Lilies (which they are not). They are very easy to grow, but are bothered however with leaf-rollers that cut good sized holes in the leaves. This may be controlled with a Chlordane dust. There are many hybrids available, some in dwarfs and some in medium sizes. A glowing pink is called HUNGARIA and RICHARD WALLACE is canary yellow. A very rich red scarlet is called the PRESIDENT. You can order them from the George W. Park Seed Co., Greenwood, S. C., the Reuter Seed Co., New Orleans, La., and local stores.

Another old-time favorite that is easy to grow and is available in old standards or newer hybrids is called "Crinum." Many are called Milk and Wine Lilies, however this name is usually applied to the types with red and white striped blossoms. There are many excellent Crinum hybrids and species available that should be included in your garden in Gulf Coast States and all of Florida. One of the most outstanding is "CECIL HOUDY-SHEL" a free-blooming type bearing large umbels of clear pink, trumpet shaped blossoms on tall stems. Another is ELLEN BOSANQUET with wine-colored blossoms. Source: BECKWITH D. SMITH, 2036 Post St., Jacksonville, Fla.

ORCHID TREE (Bauhinia variegata) — The Glory of February and March. Central Florida southward its multitude of orchid or purplish colored blossoms beautify the highways, streets, and gardens. There is a white blossom type that is also much in evidence at the same time.

Florida Planting Guide — March

Although March is considered the beginning of Spring in Florida, we generally have considerable evidence of Spring growth during much of February. Many old-timers consider the blooming of the Wild Plum (Chickasaw Plum) as the "harbinger" of Spring. The Red Bud (*Cercis canadensis L.*)and the Fringetree (*Chionanthus virginicus*) are likewise the sign of Spring. All three make excellent specimen or landscape material. The Fringetree which usually blooms a few weeks later than the plum or red bud is often called the "Old-man's-beard tree" because of the masses of white flowers with ribbon-like petals. They are slightly fragrant and are in loose drooping clusters from four to six inches long. Seldom do you find the wild plum or fringetree in the average run of nurseries in Florida, but are often found in the woods or along the roads. Because the red bud and the fringetree grow as far north as Tennessee they are often found listed in nursery catalogs out of Florida. The fringetree may be started from seeds sown the Spring or Fall. The Harry E. Saier catalog (mentioned before) lists seeds under *Chionanthus virginica*.

Sometimes a tree or plant becomes so common that it is taken for granted and left to grow without appreciation of its virtues. One such tree is the CHINABERRY (or Umbrella Tree) which was in nearly everybody's yard or farm at the turn of the century. This tree which loses its foliage in the Fall is really a beautiful sight in the Spring and most of the Summer. Masses of lavender or purplish flowers brings to mind the lilac, in fact it is called the INDIAN LILAC Tree in Asia. There is a distinctive fragrance which is very pleasant, and many hundreds of berry - like (drupe) fruits which are shades of green or yellow (more like the olive) follow. These are dried and used for making beads, however the youngsters of by-gone days had another use for them. They would make a pop-gun from the Elderberry tree branches (pulp removed leaves a hollow center) and with a little lard or grease on a plunger, it was ideal for shooting Chinaberries. This is a good tree where you have plenty of space. It makes an ideal shade for chickens or cattle or you as a matter of fact. Each Chinaberry fruit has enough seed material for a tree or two. One thing to keep in mind is that they are not edible.

* * *

Feed lawns this month. Use 100 lbs. of Special Lawn Fertilizer to each 50 x 50 area, or about four pounds per 100 square feet. Some prefer feeding with soluble type plant foods, using special guns that fit on your garden hose that are found in most garden supply stores.

* * *

Young trees need feeding at this time. Start now and feed every six weeks through June. A good time to feed citrus, if you didn't feed in January or February. Special citrus mixtures are available. An old favorite is 4-6-8 with plenty of organics. Another help that is recommended by many is applications of COLLOIDAL PHOSPHAATE around the trees, worked in slightly. It has a moisture factor that is worth much to many areas. Colloidal phosphate does have some minute amounts of trace minerals, etc., but should not be considered as a fertilizer or plant food. Some claim it makes for better flavor in citrus fruits. It is not expensive, and may be used fairly freely, or at least five pounds per large tree.

* * *

March and April is a good time to air layer CROTONS or DRACAENAS not only to get new plants, but to prevent them from becoming leggy. Air-layer plants whose top portion is symmetrical, or you may air-layer a number of the larger branches that have well-formed tops. After rooting and severing from parent plant, the lower parts will put out new growth and assume better shape.

* * *

Plant the following bulbs, rhizomes, tubers, etc., now: Amaryllis, Cannas, Achimenes, Crinums, Costus, Gloxinia, Ginger, Daylilies (Hemerocallis), Louisiana Iris, Tuberous Begonias, Ismene, Tuberoses, Rain Lilies (Zephyranthes), Fairy Lilies, Cooperia, Monbretia, Gloriosa lilies (Climbing lily), Alstroemeria, Watsonias.

* * *

LIATRIS is the name of a plant often called Gay Feather or Blazing Stars, which blooms the latter part of the Summer in Florida. There are a number of wild Liatris growing in fields along the roadsides that are admired by all, and many people use them for cut flowers. These flowers shade from lavender to purple and are in spikes or racemes. The long stems filled with flowers make a nice effect when grown in masses. It is rather difficult to start the wild Liatris, but many fine hybrids are available that are much superior, and you may obtain roots at stores, from catalogs or you may purchase the seed of many varieties. Some firms sell the plants.

* * *

March is the time to provide plant food and fertilizers for the largest majority of plants and shrubs. You have many choices in organic plant foods, soluble plant foods, dry fertilizers with organics added, or you may use stable, barnyard manures (if available). Most garden supply stores have a number of dehydrated manures such as cow or sheep manure, and many excellent composts that provide both plant food and humus.

* * *

The three major plant foods found in most commercial fertilizers or soluble plant foods are Nitrogen, Phosphorus and Potash, and the three

Florida Planting Guide — March

numbers such as 4-7-5 or 6-8-8 etc., stand for the percentages of each found in the formula. In other words 4-7-5 means 4% Nitrogen, 7% Phosphorous, and 5% Potash. To the three major foods are added a number of (from 15 to 20) minor elements, or they may be present in minute amounts along with certain other forms of the major elements used. One thing is certain, the cheaper grades of commercial fertilizers seldom have enough minor elements or the best of major elements. It pays to buy a No. 1 grade of commercial fertilizer, even if the cost is almost double. Remember, you can supplement any fertilizer or general run of plant foods with soluble type minor elements such as MINOREL, and others. Many excellent foliage sprays are on the market for this purpose.

* * *

In recent years the TRANSVAAL DAISY (Gerbera jamesoni) has undergone a transition to what is now better known as the GERBERA. The many new hybrids of this daisy-like flower are much in demand in nearly all areas of Florida. You have a wide selection of colors available in solids, pastels, etc., ranging from white to cream, pink, rose, red, orange, and in single or double flowers. Propagation is from seeds or division. If you have plants that are three years old or more, this is the time to divide them. Plant in soil that is near the neutral point . . . that is slightly alkaline or slightly acid, but is fairly rich. GERBERAS grow in large clumps and produce flowers (one to each stem) on stiff stems from six to 12 inches in length. They make excellent cut flowers for vases etc. Although you may start them from seed, it is much easier to start from divisions which are usually sold by most nurseries and garden stores.

VEGETABLES

Beans	Mustard
Beets	Okra
Cabbage	Potatoes
Cantaloupe	Pumpkin
Carrots	Radish
Collards	Roselle
Corn (Sweet)	Spinach
Cucumbers	Squash
Kale	Swiss Chard
Kohl Rabi	Tomato
Lettuce	Turnip
	Watermelon

GRASSES AND FIELD CROPS

Beans (Velvet)	Millet
Benne	Peas
Corn (Field)	Peanuts
Crotalaria	Rape
Grasses (Bermuda or Carpet seed)	Rice
Grasses (Sudan, Italian Rye or Bahia)	Egyptian Wheat
	Sorghum
Indigo	Sunflower
Hegari	Trigonella (Fenugreek)

PLANTING GUIDE — FLOWERS

Ageratum	Impatiens (Sultana)
Alyssum	Ipomoea (Morning Glories)
Amaranthus	
Arctotis (Blue-eyed Afr. Daisy)	Kochia (Summer Cypress)
Aster	Lantana
Aubrietia (Rock Cress)	Marigold
	Morning Glory
Bachelor Button	Moon Vine
Balloon Vine	Nemophila (Baby Blue Eyes)
Balsam (Touch Me Nots)	
	Nigella
Brachycome	Petunia
Browallia	Portulaca
Calliopsis	Salvia
Campanula	Scabiosa
Carnation	Sweet William
Celosia (Cockscomb)	Thunbergia (Alata or fragrans)
Cleome (Spider Plant)	
Chrysanthemum	Thunbergia (Clock Vine)
Coreopsis	
Cosmos	Tithonia
Dahlia	Torenia (Summer Pansies)
Didiscus (Blue Lace Flower)	
	Verbena
Four O'Clock	Vinca (Periwinkle)
Gaillardia	Zinnia
Geum	
Globe Amaranth	FLOWERING VINES:
Gilia	
Godetia	Cypress Vine
Gourds	Balloon Vine
Helichrysum (Strawflower)	Morning Glories
	Moon Vine
Helianthus (Sunflower)	Thunbergias
Heliotrope	Passion Flowers (Red, Blue, White, Pink)
Hollyhock	

Field of Coreopsis — Brilliant yellow daisy-like flowers.

Florida Planting Guide — April

Now is the time to prune the largest majority of shrubs, especially Crotons, Hibiscus and Poinsettias. Be sure to give a generous feeding after pruning is finished. It is a good time to start cuttings of many plants, and you use some of the material for that purpose. Make Poinsettia cuttings from 10 to 12 inches long, and root them in one of the mediums discussed under Propagation. Sharp builders sand with soluble plant food is excellent.

* * *

This is a good time to reshape the Powder Puff shrub (Calliandra) and it also is a good time to air-layer them for larger plants in a hurry. They also start from cuttings, but air-layering is preferred by most growers.

* * *

You may also air-layer Crotons, Hibiscus and other shrubs and trees at this time. One flowering tree that responds most easily to this method is the HIBISCUS TREE (Hibiscus tiliaceaus) or its close relative, the Cuban Bast.

* * *

Crotons should be fed every month from now until October. If you use soluble type plant foods, it usually takes two good feedings a month during the summer. For that extra brilliant color, give a good spraying (foliage feeding) of Minorel or Sequestrene every six weeks. The general garden fertilizer with plenty of organics is also good for Crotons.

* * *

This is a good time to apply mulches to many plants. One of the easiest mulches to obtain is grass clippings that have been allowed to stand long enough to look as though they were dried-out or yellowish. If you have any of the Mother's Tongue (Albizzia lebbek) trees on your place or nearby, those pesky seed pods (as some call them) may be piled and left a few weeks, then be used as a mulch. They may be mixed too with other materials. Well matured sawdust or shavings are excellent mulch material, but if you use them, be sure and incorporate additional organic nitrogen to the soil. Milorganite, Castro Pomace Sludge, and others may be used.

* * *

This is the month that most of the insects, pests, etc., begin to show up in numbers. For instance those pesky worms appear on the yellow flowering shrubs like *Cassia beareana, Cassia bicapsularis or Simea* and others of the same group, and look like part of the foliage or flowers. Spray with arsenate of lead. Don't use any chlordane formula for this type, as it will cause the leaves to turn yellow and drop.

One of the smallest pests is a minute slender insect known as THRIPS, and they come in a variety of colors such as yellow, brown, black and perhaps others. They suck the plant juices causing them to have faded or whitish blotches, and when they become numerous there is considerable browning and withering of foliage, and even distorted buds. Many of the buds fail to open or open only partially. For control use Rose Dusts, End-O-Pests, Red Arrow or Isotox and similar formulas.

* * *

April and May are two bad months for fleas, and if you have cats or dogs or no pets at all, you may have a yard infested with these pests. Remember that fleas transmit typhus, plague and tularemia, and are a host of the tape-worm. They can be exterminated by using wettable material such as BHC 12% at the rate of one pound for 500 to 800 square feet, or you may use 1% Lindane Dust or 5% DDT dust at the rate of one pound to cover 100 square feet.

* * *

This is the time to feed roses, and remember they are heavy feeders, so give each plant a handful of a good rose fertilizer per plant every month. You mustn't neglect the spraying or dusting if you want plants free from mildew, blackspot, and other diseases or pests. Most rose dusts take care of many things, but be sure and read directions.

* * *

In your garden these need plant food at this time: Citrus, Ixoras, Azaleas, Camellias, Hibiscus, Jasmines, Palms, Lawns, Grapes, Java Plum, Hydrangeas, Pentas, and most other plants that show new growth just starting.

* * *

Give a light application of fertilizer to AVOCADOS at this time. Spray bloom and young fruit with a Copper Fungicide spray.

* * *

A good time to set out the following vines: Clematis (Northern parts), Thunbergia grandiflora, fragrans or alata (also called Black-eyed Susan vine), Hoya Carnosa, Wisteria and Honeysuckle.

* * *

The following plants may be set out: Phlox Drummondi, Verbena, Chrysanthemum, Coleus, Begonia, Sempervivum, Celosia, Amaranthus, Impatiens, African Daisies, Anchusa, Petunias, Salvia, Stokesia, Perennial Phlox. Many others for your area may be found at your local garden supply houses or nurseries.

Florida Planting Guide — April

CALADIUMS are one of the most colorful of foliage plants for shady nooks, beds in partial sun or shady areas, or to grow in pots, tubs, etc. It is a favorite in Florida and other warm areas for patio urns. You may buy them already started, or you can purchase bulbs of a multitude of patterns, colors, etc. They are seldom bothered with insects or disease, and once planted you can practically forget about them, however a feeding or a soluble plant food now and then will reward you with better color and general appearance. If you plant them outside or in containers, remember they like plenty of organic material in the soil or mixture. Most garden supply places have composts, or mixtures suitable for the purpose. In most parts of Florida they may be left in the soil from year to year. The foliage will die down in the colder months, but will come back with the warm weather.

* * *

Besides Caladiums, you may plant the following bulbs this month: Gladiolus, Tuberose, Tuberous Begonias (under some conditions), Ismene Calathina (Peruvian Daffodil), Wild and Louisana Iris, Achimenes, Ginger, Dahlias, Cannas, Callus, Cooperia, Crinum, Costus spec., Hemerocallis.

* * *

You may also plant Billbergia nutans, Aechmeas, other Bromeliads, and other plants that produce plantlets, suckers, offsets, rosettes such as Echeveria, Sempervivum, (Hen and Chickens), Anthericum, Aloes, Marica, and the Pineapple. There are hundreds of others that do well in Florida.

* * *

If you really want flowers most of the summer, don't forget the many hundreds of Zinnias, Marigolds, Cosmos, and Petunias. The hybrids on the market of all these favorite garden flowers actually run into thousands. Besides those found in the general run of seed packets on display, there are many more obtainable from seed specialists mentioned on other pages of this book.

The Palm Leaf Miner infests many of the palms in the Phoenix group. When the fronds show brown patches that gradually turn yellow and die, and the heavy midribs are found in a shredded condition filled with small worms, bits of web and debris, you had better be on guard, for there are five generations a year. A night flying moth lays eggs directly on the leaf bud of the young leaflets. The worms feed in colonies of thirty or more under a fine silken web. For control use a dust containing Chlordane (like Marchlor) or a spray like ISOTOX. Apply well down in the fronds.

That sooty mold found on so many plants is caused by WHITE FLIES which are small white winged insects usually found in large numbers on the foliage of plants like the Gardenia, Citrus, Ligustrum, Java Plum and other Eugenias, Privet,

Viburnum, Confederate Rose (*Hibiscus mutabilis*), Crepe Myrtle, Avocado, Mango, Loquat, and hundreds of others. This sooty appearance is taken on by many plants in nearby areas. Ants seem to spread the honey-dew excreted by whiteflies. This unsightly sooty mold keeps growing and spoils the ornamental value of all plants infested. Although there are many variations of the Whitefly, that is they have such names as Citrus Whitefly, Azalea Whitefly, etc., they all cause about the same damage and may be controlled by the same kind of sprays. Most authorities recommend sprays that contain oil with lindane (LINOIL), or with nicotine sulphate, and other ingredients. Florida Volck is one brand well suited for Citrus. It is applied when the fruit is about the size of marbles.

* * *

For that sooty mold on Gardenias, one gardener had wonderful results using the juice from pickles (any kind) mixed with water and poured over the foliage. Just save the juice from your jars of pickles and fill with water to the top and pour over bushes at intervals of two weeks. What falls to the soil seems to be good for extra acidity needed by Gardenias. This may work on other acid-loving plants. Some people throw the old wash-water over the foliage and it often helps remove that dirty, gummy appearance caused by whiteflies.

* * *

Daylilies should be at their height this month and next month in most areas. This is a good time to select new ones for your garden. Although they will transplant almost anytime, it is better to do this in the Fall. Large clumps will take better at this time.

WHITE GINGER LILY — Hedychium also called Butterfly Lily - very fragrant - other colors available.

Florida Planting Guide — April

APRIL FLOWERS

Amaranthus
Aster
Bachelor Button
Balloon Vine
Balsam (Touch
　Me Not)
Calliopsis
Chrysanthemum
Correopsis
Castor Bean
Cleome (Spider Plant)
Cosmos
Dahlia
Dianthus (Pinks)
Four O'Clock
Gaillardia
Gilia
Globe Amaranth
Gourds
Helianthus (Sunflower)
Marigold

Morning Glory
Moonflower Vine
Portulaca
Salvia
Safflower
Sultana
Sunflower
Rudbeckia (Golden
　Glow)
Tithonia
Torenia (Summer
　Pansies)
Verbena
Vinca (Periwinkle)
Zinnia
FLOWERING VINES:
Balloon Vine,
Cypress Vine
Morning Glories
Moonflower
Thunbergias

GRASSES AND FIELD SEEDS

Beans (Velvet
Beggarweed
Benne
Chufas
Clover (Alyce)
Corn (Field)
Crotalaria
Grasses (Bermuda,
　Carpet, Italian Rye,
　Sudan, Bahia)

Indigo
Hegari
Millet
Peanuts
Rice
Wheat (Egyptian)
Sorghum
Sunflower

VEGETABLES

Beans
Cantaloupe
Collard
Mustard
Okra
Pumpkin

Radish
Roselle
Spinach
Turnip
Watermelon

STOKESIA (Stokes Aster). Bluish to purple aster-like flowers.
May be divided every two years.

Aechmea Minata discolor (Bromelaid family). Easy to grow
in soil or up in air either in hanging baskets or recesses in
trees. Very brilliant red flowers with blue petals. Produces
many suckers or sprouts from old base.

ALOE VERA—One of the most useful plants for treatment
of burns, mosquito bites, ulcers, and as a face cream. Leaves
contain a clear mucilaginous substance that is rubbed on the
skin. It multiplies by suckers—grows in the shade.

Not too many flowers and plants for this month, however, there are always sufficient numbers and varieties that can be started from seeds and, of course, a number of started plants can be obtained from your source of supply. For instance, there is a delightful plant that produces many small pansy-like blossoms called TORENIA, and which can be started from seeds or transplants. They usually come up every year once they have been established. Torenia is known by many as either the Wishbone plant or Summer Pansies. It reaches about a foot in height and is covered with many white and lavender flowers with yellow blotches, and does have a slight resemblance to a pansy. It is a very sun-tolerant plant that may be used in edgings, borders, or for the rock garden. It often re-seeds and many new plants are found each year.

* * *

Another colorful flower which is ideal for the hot summer months is one called TITHONIA or the Golden Flower of the Incas (Mexico). There are some hybrids that do have golden flowers (like small sunflowers), however most have a vermillion or orange color. You may plant the seeds now right where you want them to grow and by summer they will reach from six to eight feet in height. They make excellent cut flowers as well as enhancing the landscape.

* * *

The COMPOSITE family is one of the largest in the plant world with over 800 widely dispersed genera of herbs, shrubs, etc., and whose flowers are more or less like a daisy. There are hundreds of garden flowers in this big family that we are familiar with and perhaps some of the easiest to grow. The list includes Ageratum, Arctotis, Aster, Calendula, Centaurea, Coreopsis, Cosmos, Chrysanthemums, Dahlias, Strawflowers, Liatris, Sunflower, Tithonia, Stokesia, Zinnia, Marigolds, etc. Of this list you can plant Cosmos, Coreopsis, Marigolds, Zinnias, Tithonia. Most composites do not require soil that is too fertile, in fact you often see fields or masses of Cosmos and Coreopsis growing in sandy areas all over Florida and the Southland.

You can can also plant the seeds of the various members of the AMARANTH family, especially the Celosias or Cockscombs. Bachelor Buttons. The Molten Fire Amaranthus. and also Joseph Coat Amaranthus may be planted in North Florida, but they do better if planted in February or March. You will find a large list of Celosias in seed catalogs. There are some that have plumy type heads, some with compact heads, and others with heads of the crested type and resembling a cock's comb. In the plumy types you can get a variety of colors and tints, especially the yellow, gold, and red. The plumes can be dried and used for decorations and arrangements. Here is how

IXORA — Glory of the Summer, April until October.

to prepare them; select well-developed blooms, and clip before color starts fading. Remove leaves and stems and hang upside down in a cool airy place in the shade. When stem is dry, they are ready for use, and will last a long time.

* * *

You can still plant a few bulbs this month. This list includes Ismene, or Peruvian Daffodil, Monbretia, Watsonias, Zephyranthes, Rain Lilies, Habranthus, Cooperias, Hymenocallis (Spider Lilies), Lycoris Aurea the Golden Hurricane Lily. Cannas, Narcissus, Achimenes.

* * *

There are many packaged bulbs sold in the dime stores, department stores, and stores who handle garden items, that include bulbs not especially suited for your area. Some for instance like the Rubrum Lily may grow in northern limits of Florida, but fail in Central and South Florida. Now and then you will find some of the bulbs for colder areas growing and showing up well for a spell, however the chances are slight. We all like to experiment, so perhaps you might succeed with the hard-to-grow or forbidden plants. Remember that Tulips of certain kinds now grow in Florida, and they were once on the forbidden list.

* * *

A living mulch growing under trees and shrubs is a good thing sometimes, providing the mulch plants do not take too much plant food. Experiments have shown that the BRYOPHYLLUM PINNATA (*Kalanchoe pinnata*) growing around the AVOCADO helped the yield considerably. This is a very common plant often sold in curio shops or plant departments as an Air Plant, Life-Plant. or Lucky Leaf (and many other such names). Anyway if you can obtain a few leaves, by the end of the season or year you will have thick growth around trees or shrubs. Some flower around the holidays. Most of the Bryophyllum or small Kalanchoe plants are surface feeders and can easily be pulled up if necessary.

The Yellow Allamanda is perhaps one of the most popular flowering shrubs of the Summer months. It grows easily in all areas from the middle of Central Florida to the Keys. Some have luck with them in parts of North Florida. They respond to any good garden fertilizer. Don't like wet feet, so provide good drainage. There is also an allamanda that is commonly called the Purple Allamanda, however the color is more dusky rose or has shades of violet. The Cryptostegia (also called Rubber Vine) is called Purple Allamanda by many, however it is not even related. It may be grown in same manner and place or intermixed with the true purple and brilliant yellow types. Either plant starts easily from cuttings in Spring or Fall and is seldom bothered with insects or pests, however aphids do attack now and then.

MAY — FLOWERS

Aster	Morning Glory
Bachelor Button	Portulaca
Balloon Vine	Salvia
Balsam	Safflower
Cosmos	Sunflower
Cleome (Spider Plant)	Thunbergias
Dahlia	Tithonias
Digitalis (Foxglove)	Torenia
Four O'Clock	Vinca (Periwinkle)
Gaillardia	Zinnia
Gilia	Balloon Vine
Gourds	Cypress Vine
Helianthus (Sunflower)	Moonflower Vine
Marigold	Thunbergias.
Mignonette	

Purple (Magenta) Allamanda — not as prolific as yellow type, but very effective in garden or landscape.

Yellow Allamanda (Brown Bud) one of the most popular flowering shrubs for all Florida except extreme northern areas. Easily started from cuttings.

Purple Cryptostegia— (Rubber Vine) often called purple Allamanda. Mixes with yellow.

VEGETABLES

Beans (Pole)
Collards
Mustard
Okra
Pumpkin
Spinach

GRASSES AND FIELD SEEDS

Beans (Velvet)
Beggarweed
Benne

Chufas
Clover (Alyce)
Corn (Field)
Crotalaria
Grasses, (Bermuda, Carpet)
Grasses, (Italian Rye, Sudan, Bahia)
Indigo
Hegari
Millet
Peas
Peanuts
Sesbania
Wheat (Egyptian)
Sorghum
Sunflower

WHITE BAUHINIA — Bauhinia Acuminata. Small bush-type plant and a free bloomer most of year.

Florida Planting Guide — June

ROYAL POINCIANA — Most spectacular of all flowering trees in Florida. The Glory of June-July. Long seed pods form within 8 to 12 months. Seeds keep for years. Flowers are from deep orange to deep red color.

By June most gardeners suffer from "Inertia" which is the scientific name for laziness. It is too hot to do much work in the open, however we must do a little or the garden will go to pot. If you insist on planting seed now, include most of the Composites mentioned for May, and you might include a few more such as Calliopsis, Gaillardia, Rudbeckia, Arctotis and Stokesia. There is a small strawflower known as Acrolinium that may be planted now. They produce a variety of colors and patterns in their straw-like flowers, and they may be used as cut-flowers or as dried bouquets. You can plant them in front of the Helichrysum type strawflowers which grow much taller and have larger flowers.

You may plant single or double flowered Coreopsis at this time. They are ideal for mass effects in borders or in fields or along fence rows. Cosmos is also suited for the same purpose. A number of hybrids are available. Still another one for the same purpose is the old familiar Blanket Flower known as Gaillardia. They are now available in double flower forms.

If you didn't plant Tithonia in April or May, you still have a chance to get late Summer blooms by planting now. Same applies for Torenia, Cleome Portulaca, Morning-Glories, Balsam, Four-O'Clocks, Nicotiana and Verbena.

Azaleas take on a certain bareness after the season is well over, so why not plant Caladiums or English Ivy among the bushes to help the beauty of the landscape.

The Coral Vine (*Antiginon leptopus*) is usually in bloom at this time all over Florida. Although this vine produces many seeds (which may be set aside for later planting), they also produce tubers after the first year growth. These tubers produce better plants much quicker than from seed. You do not always find them listed on the market, but I notice them in the catalog of H. G. Hastings Co. of Atlanta, Ga. Most people that have a number of vines growing will be glad to give you tubers, but most really don't know they are in the ground on old plants. In Texas they have a white (instead of pink) flowering Coral Vine (if you can still call it by that name).

Good time to obtain cuttings or plants of the various Chrysanthemums. By October you should have many fine flowers for cutting or corsages.

If bees or other pollinating insects are scarce, you can help the yield of flowers or fruit by spraying with NAPH or BLOSSOM SET. Sometimes a spraying of NAPH will help prevent buddrop on Hibiscus and other plants.

Well established lawns should be fertilized at this time. One of the quickest ways to get your lawn green is to spray it with a soluble type plant food like Nutrisol, Cypress Gardens Plant Food, Hygro or others of like nature.

A perennial vine that bears deep blue sweetpea-like blossoms is called CLITORIA, and it may be started from seed at this time. There is a single and a double flowered type, and sometimes it is possible to get seeds of a pink-flowered Clitoria. A trellis with both the pink Coral Vine and the double-flowered Clitoria is really a beautiful sight.

June is a good month to transplant trees and shrubs, especially if there is sufficient rainfall. Ideal time also to plant palms.

Gardenias should be about through with blooming, so you may prune them enough to shape them. Good time to pinch your Poinsettias to keep them from getting leggy.

Now is the proper time to start lawns from seed. Give the soil a generous amount of organic fertilizer like Scott's Turf Builder, Milorganite, Castor-Pomace or sludge. Sow the seed and cover lightly with washed sand. Colloidal phosphate added to the soil and worked in will help hold the moisture and provide a minute amount of minerals.

Papaya fly and web worms may be prevalent now, they can be controlled with DDT spray. For powdery mildew use sulphur dust or spray.

You can plant the following herbs in June and July: Anise, Borage, Cress, Summer Savory, Thyme, Dill, Lavender, Rosemary, Basil, Chervil, Sage, Marjoram.

Crepe Myrtles (*Lagerstroemia indica*) have the reputation of having the longest blooming season of any tree in the South. They are in bloom in most areas of Florida at this time. Watermelon pink, and other pinks and red, whites, and lavender or purple colors may be found among the plantings. Some cities are famous for Crepe Myrtle. Tallahassee has many hundreds. Feed them with 5-10-5 using about two pounds per tree in latter part of May or even in June. Mildew often attacks the young leaves. Dust with sulphur or any good rose-dust. As soon as your blossoms have finished blooming, cut them off and you will get the second bloom and sometimes the third bloom. They lose their leaves in Fall and Winter, so it is a good idea to back them up with an evergreen shrub or tree. Propagate from softwood cuttings in Summer, or hardwood cuttings in Fall or Spring.

Florida Planting Guide — July

This is the month of increased laziness and neglect, however there is usually much to do, if so inclined. This is a good time to consider mulching of many plants, and believe it or not there is much available material if you look around. We have already mentioned sawdust, shavings, grass clippings, seed pods like the Mothers Tongue Tree, oak leaves, and several other items, but you may add to this list the following: Java Plum (*Eugenia jambolana*) leaves, pine needles, seaweed, water-lily pads, (Hyacinths), peanut hulls, moss from fresh water ponds or lakes, pine bark broken in small pieces. Don't forget the living mulches such as Bryophyllum or Kalanchoe mentioned last month. Many ground covers may be used for this purpose. North Florida and South Georgia nurserymen use pine bark for camellias and azaleas.

* * *

One plant that might be considered in July is the "Firecracker Bush" correctly called *Russelia juncea* (*or equisetiformis*). This willowy drooping shrub is also called the Fountain-Plant because of the manner of growth. The flowers however do resemble small red fire-crackers slightly, and hence the common name of the plant. They appear in clusters. This shrub is easily divided and transplanted. Be sure and include sufficient roots when dividing or separating from parent plant.

* * *

Crepe Myrtles should be in good bloom all over Central and North Florida, and you may extend the bloom by cutting off all blooms that have finished. Sometimes it is possible to do this twice in a season. If blossoms are allowed to set seed, they will not bloom again until next season. If troubled with powdery mildew, dust with sulphur.

Any seeds that have formed on your Daylilies, Amaryllis or Crinums, Zephyranthes (Rain Lilies), Habranthus can be planted now. One of the best mediums is well matured sawdust treated with a soluble plant food. Daylilies seeds should be planted as soon as ripe, as they don't keep very long (seldom over three or four months) and every month you delay you will lose a large percentage. Iris and gladiolus seeds too may be planted as soon as they are ripe.

Azaleas and Camellias should have their summer feeding at this time. Use any good Azalea and Camellia Special fertilizer. Apply on top of summer mulch and water in. Do not cultivate around azaleas or camellias. Pull up weeds, etc. For thrip, red spider and lace wing bug spray with ISOTOX Garden Spray M.

Keep on the lookout for the small moth that lays the eggs of army and sod webworms. When they are present in large numbers, give your lawn two sprayings of Ortho Lawn Spray, Diben or DDT, with applications seven to 10 days apart.

* * *

This is perhaps the next best month to give the last pruning to Poinsettias. Cut back about half the growth made since March. This will give you more and better blooms later. Some prefer August for this chore.

* * *

You may plant seeds of winter - flowering vines, such as the Argyrea (large leaf silvery and woolly underneath), or those started from cuttings may be planted now. This includes the Flame Vine (Pyrostegia), and the Porana (blooms in November), often called Snow Creeper.

A very beautiful flowering vine that is a mass of white flowers in December and sometimes into January is one known as *Ipomea sidaefolia*. The flowers look like a small edition of the moonflower. It forms many seeds that ripen in the summer, and may set out any time. This vine becomes very woody in time, but its gnarled twisted wood is an excellent substitute for certain driftwoods. Not recommended for North Florida.

* * *

Rooted chrysanthemums are available now, and should be planted in cans or pots. Inquire at garden stores or nurseries.

This is the height of the Mango season, and usually the month for showing the best varieties at the annual exhibition of the Florida Mango Forum. If you want to know more about the Mango, send for the bulletin "Mangos in Florida" by S. John Lynch and Margaret Mustard, obtainable from your County agent, or the Florida State Dept. of Agriculture, Tallahassee, Fla.

FIRECRACKER BUSH (Russelia Juncea). A willowy shrub that is excellent for Central and South Florida, and which bears scarlet red flowers.

Florida Planting Guide — August

Vacations are either over or just starting for the average gardener in Florida, August is a sort of "in-between" month and more or less a time to plan or to prepare for the full swing into fall gardening which usually starts about the middle of September.

* * *

You can clean up those old flower-pots or containers by using two or three tablespoonsful of Clorox in a gallon of water. Soak the pots for 24 hours. Scrub them down with a stiff brush.

* * *

If your soil is mostly filled-in sand, or if you live close to the seacoast, it is a good idea to incorporate some Colloidal Phosphate into the top two to four inches of soil. If you plant shrubs and trees, then place two or three or even as much as five pounds in the planting hole. The larger the plant the more Colloidal Phosphate. Mix it with good rich soil or compost.

This is the time to prune Allamandas, Durantas (Golden Dewdrop), Ixoras (Flame of the Woods), and Hibiscus (not too much at this time). The Rubber Vine is rightly Cryptostegia but often called purple Allamanda (which is incorrect for there is a true purple one). It is the shrub that produces many purplish flowers along with the Allamandas and should not be pruned until the limbs have dried enough not to emit a milky-fluid. This sometimes runs up into October or November. You may even wait until after the cold weather. The seed pods (which are huge) take almost a year to ripen then they will burst open and reveal many silky seeds that are easy to germinate.

* * *

Many bulbous or tuberous type plants can be divided now and in September. Divide Amaryllis, Hemerocallis (Daylilies), and Crinums. Dahlias set out at this time will flower in Autumn in North Florida.

Crepe Myrtle should be finished blooming and the flower heads should be cut off and not allowed to go to seed.

* * *

Gladiolus planted now will produce flowers within three months. Plant every two or three weeks to extend the flowering season.

This is the last chance to cut back your Poinsettias, if you haven't done so. Do this before August 20th.

* * *

Pansies sown during August will produce well established plants for Fall planting. Sow seeds in flats containing half and half coarse builders sand and Vermiculite (or Perlite), or you may use shredded spaghnum moss over sharp sand. Treat with a nutrient solution made by dissolving one teaspoon soluble plant food in a gallon of water.

* * *

Many nurseries and garden shops still have boxes of Chrysanthemums available. A good time to get them for home or garden.

* * *

The bean hamper or can method of growing plants in shavings make it possible to grow many plants now that wouldn't survive or do well in soil. Tomatoes, peppers, cucumbers, and even honey-dew melons have been grown in full sun and ripened during July, August and September. See chapter on Hydroponic gardening.

* * *

Now is a good time to send for your Fall seed catalogs and to order seeds for planting in September, October and November.

* * *

Many of the Gloriosa lilies have produced seed pods by now. Leave them on the vines until they burst open, then gather seeds and plant later. They need a ripening period before planting, so you can keep them for a year if you like. Sow seeds in sawdust, or any of the mixtures mentioned in first part of this book.

Plant all the Daylily seeds that have ripened. Remember they lose every month you keep them, in fact after six months the chances of germination are slim. Most seed pods are ripe when they turn brown or slightly brown or if they break open.

Many vegetables can be planted the latter part of August, this includes field peas, snap-beans, cucumbers, okra, mustard, summer squash, and tomatoes. For Central and South Florida mostly.

FLORIDA PLANTING CALENDER FOR JUNE — JULY — AUGUST

JUNE FLOWERS

Aster	Tithonia
Cleome	Vinca (Periwinkle)
Cosmos	Zinnia
Dahlia	VEGETABLES:
Four O'Clock	Collard
Gaillardia	Eggplant
Helianthus (Sunflower)	Mustard
Marigold	Okra
Morning Glory	Pepper
Portulaca	Rutabaga
Salvia	Spinach
Safflower	Turnip
Sunflower	

JULY FLOWERS

Aster	Marigold
Cleome	Sunflower
Cosmos	Vinca (Periwinkle)
Gaillardia	Zinnia

GRASSES AND FIELD CROPS

Beans (Velvet)	VEGETABLES:
Beggarweed	Celery
Chufas	Collards
Corn	Eggplant
Cowpeas	Mustard
Hegari	Okra
Millet	Pepper
Grasses (Bermuda,	Rutabaga
Sudan, Bahia)	Spinach
	Turnip

AUGUST FLOWERS

Aubrietia (Rock Cress)	Sunflower
Cleome	Sweet William
Cosmos	Verbena
Gaillardia	Vinca (Periwinkle)
Helianthus (Sunflower)	Zinnia
Marigold	

VEGETABLES

Broccoli	Mustard
Brussel Sprouts	Okra
Cabbage	Onion Sets
Cauliflower	Pepper
Celery	Radish
Collard	Romaine
Cucumber	Rutabaga
Eggplant	Spinach
Endive	Squash
Garlic	Tomato
Kale	Turnip
Lettuce	

GRASSES AND FIELD SEEDS

Cowpeas	Grasses (Bermuda,
Millet	Sudan, Bahia)
Sunflower	

CREPE MYRTLE — Longest blooming season of any flowering tree in Florida.

Plumeria — Frangipani, popular tree-like shrub with thick soft branches. Milky sap. Fragrant flowers. White, Pink, and variegated. Grow best in South Florida.

Florida Planting Guide — September

We think of this month as the beginning of the Fall gardening season, and most gardeners realize it is time to do almost everything in the garden category. This includes the soil preparation, the raking, burning, piling, moving of pruned limbs, leaves, weeds and a host of other items on the labor side. Then comes the layout of beds, the planting of seeds or transplants or established plants. I might add this is also the time that your garden supply man has a very happy look on his face.

* * *

A list of suggested annuals, perennials and vegetables follows. However, no list is complete because of many factors — weather, soil, conditions of your area, and the new or imported items that keep appearing. Also, many improved hybrids will grow in areas or under conditions that would not support them before.

When you go through the catalogs of the Parks Seed Company (or Burgess, or others) you realize how many hundreds of flowers, shrubs and trees are available for you to try in your garden.

* * *

If you don't bother with starting seeds or bulbs, etc., you can always find the many standard seedlings or transplants at your garden supply houses or nurseries.

* * *

Usually the first roses appear on the market during September, and a good many are waxed or storage roses, and although some of them will grow, it is best to wait until October, November or December to plant the better ones that are then available. California and New York State, and Texas all have some good roses for your selection. Thomasville, Georgia produces excellent roses for Florida growing which are not waxed.

* * *

You will get larger and better blooms from your Chrysanthemums if you will pinch off the flower buds now. Watch for signs of mildew, mites, blackspot, etc. Many good dusts are available that will control these pests.

Good time to divide and dig GERBERAS. Remember that they don't flourish in soil that is too sour or acid, but more or less near the neutral point. A degree or two either way would not hinder their growth. A bit of dolomite will usually correct the too-acid condition. Examine the roots before transplanting for any sign of root-knot which are deformities along the root system that look like knots and are very detrimental to future growth and perhaps to other plants nearby.

* * * *

One of the finest strawberries in years for Florida is called the Fla. No. 90. They are very large and tapered and extremely prolific. The flavor is the very best. Plants or runners are available at many supply houses now and next month. They do well also when planted in sawdust or shavings and fed with such plant foods as Nutrisol, Hy-Gro, or Perfect Plant Foods.

* * *

September and October are the bulbs and tuberous rooted months, and there is a long list of such plants that may be put in the ground during this period. Easter lilies for instance, must be planted now in order to be ready for Easter. The larger bulbs are best and more likely to bloom in time. There are a number of Easter lilies on the market such as the Croft Lily, Bermuda Easter Lily, Creole, and the Florida Easter lily or *Lilium longiflorum Floridii*. The last one is best for Florida soils and climate. Many thousands are raised in the vicinity of Sebring and Lake Placid. Do not use manures under Easter lilies and other bulbous plants.

This is really a good time to plant Daylilies, or to divide the large clumps.

* * *

This is the time that most Hibiscus start their Fall blooming period which lasts thru December. Also a good time to make your selection, as most nurseries have plants in containers and with many blooms.

By this time most of the Mallows and Hybrids have set seed, and it is a good time to gather them for planting in December or January. See chapter on Hibiscus relatives.

Florida Planting Guide — September

SEPTEMBER FLOWERS

Acrolinium (Small Strawflower)
Anchusia
Ageratum
Alyssum
Arctotis (Blue-eyed Afr. Daisy)
Aster
Aubrietia (Rock Cress)
Browallia (Amethyst)
Calendula
Calliopsis
Campanula
Candytuft
Carnation
Celosia
Centaurea
Correopsis
Cynoglossum (Chi. Forget Me Not)
Dianthus (Pinks)
Didiscus (Blue Lace Flower)
Eschscholtzia (Calif. Poppy)
Gaillardia
Godetia

Gypsophila (Baby's Breath)
Helichrysum (Strawflower)
Helianthus (Sunflower)
Hollyhock
Lantana
Lobelia
Leptosyne
Lupin
Marigold
Myosotis (Forget Me Not)
Nasturtium
Nemophila (Baby Blue Eyes)
Oenothera (Evening Primrose)
Pansy
Petunia
Phlox
Pyrethrum (Painted Daisy)
Queen Anne's Lace
Scabiosa
Schizanthus
Shasta Daisy
Snapdragon

Statice
Stocks
Sweet Peas
Sweet William

Sweet Sultan
Verbena
Vinca (Periwinkle)
Viola

VEGETABLES

Beans
Beets
Broccoli
Brussel Sprouts
Cabbage
Cauliflower
Celery
Collard
Cucumber
Endive
Garlic
Kale
Kohl Rabi
Leek
Lettuce
Mustard

Okra
Onion Seed
Onion Sets
Parsley
Parsnip
Peas, English
Radish
Rhubarb
Romaine
Spinach
Rutabaga
Squash
Swiss Chard
Tomato
Turnip

GRASSES AND FIELD SEEDS

Sweet Clover
Rye

Lupines (Kenland Red)
Grasses (Bermuda, Bahia)

GOLDEN RAIN TREE IN FULL BLOOM — Medium- fast growing tree suitable for nearly all areas of Florida.
Panicles of bright yellow change to rose-pink bladder-like bracts. Blooms from September to October.

What we didn't finish or start in September can in most cases be done this month. In other words, just about everything in the category of Fall gardening comes in September and October. The slight difference in weather between North and South Florida makes a difference of two to four weeks for certain flowers, vegetables, trees, shrubs or vines.

* * *

This is a good time to put out seedlings or transplants that were started back in August or September, especially if they have their true leaves (usually four), or if they are potted plants from a nursery or garden supply house. If the weather is real hot, it is a good idea to shade the more or less touchy plants, and an ideal item for this is the leaves or fans from palmettos. When sowing seeds in open ground at this time, it is a good idea to make a trench about an inch and a half and fill it with a good compost (granulated preferred) or even a good grade of potting soil. This helps hold the moisture for germination and for maintenance of the newly sprouted seedlings or for started transplants. Cover with ordinary top soil.

* * *

Still a good time to divide or separate Day-lilies and Amaryllis, or to set out new ones. This applies to many other bulbs or tubers.

* * *

Prune and shape spring-flowering hedges at this time. Also good time to prune Hydrangeas. You may prune broad-leaf evergreens and decidous plants enough to shape them.

It should be about the end of the Caladium season, and the wilted appearance indicates they are thru until next season. They may be lifted and replanted in other places or they may be left where they have been growing. If you want to store some of the bulbs, then let them dry in open air for a spell and then store in vermiculite, dry sand or sawdust. Plastic bags are excellent for the purpose.

Do not use oil sprays on citrus at this time, as it may cause the fruit not to ripen properly.

* * *

This is Sweet Pea time and you will be rewarded with highly fragrant flowers later, if you take proper care in soil preparation, provide sufficient plant food, and use good seeds. Sweet Peas are generally divided into two types, the early blooming Spencer variety which should be planted at this time, and the Cuthbertson variety which is planted later in the season. Spencers produce one or two flowers on short stems, while the Cuthbertson variety produces four blooms on long stems and blooms in the Spring. Even though the Spencers are called early Winter blooming Sweet Peas, some seed suppliers offer them as either early or late Spencers, and also there is Ruffled Spencer with wavy and ruffled petals. Some available named Spencers include Balls Orange improved,

Hope, Lavanda, Mars, Mrs. Herbert Hoover, Shirley Temple, Rainbow mixture, Zvolanek's Multi-flowered mixture (See Kilgore catalog). What about fertilizer for Sweet Peas? Some have success with bone meal and sheep manure mixed into beds about eight inches deep. If still available the product known as COLD SMOKE is excellent. A good compost is excellent, but should be made slightly alkaline by sprinkling some lime while the trench is being filled. You may use compost and soluble plant food and get good results. The open planting rows should be about four inches deep, but plant seed only one inch deep and two inches apart. As the plants begin to grow you may fill in the original four inch trench or row until it eventually becomes even with the ground. Thin out the weak plants so that you will have the healthiest ones spaced from four to eight inches apart. A trellis must be provided for vines to grow on, and this can be poultry netting, mesh netting, or similar material. Mulching is also recommended after the plants are well established and starting to climb. Keep blooms cut to prevent setting seed and also reducing number of blooms. If the stems get short, you may apply Nitrate of Soda at the rate of one tablespoon to each gallon of water. Aphids can be controlled with Isoxtox Spray and spider mites with dusting sulphur or Kelthane.

* * *

Another climbing plant that produces many beautiful flowers for cutting, and etc., is the Nasturtium. Some of the dwarf types are effective for beds, borders and general landscape.. Plant either type where they are to grow, and sow the seed about an inch and a half deep, and from eight to 24 inches apart. Nasturtiums do well in poor to medium soil. They do not like too much plant food or humus.

* * *

Time to plant rye grass in order to keep that green apearance in your lawn or bare places. It will not hurt your regular lawn, and will not turn brown as most grasses do with cold weather. Rye grass will germinate in about 10 days if watered a little every day. Five pounds of seed will cover approximately 1,000 square feet on established lawns. For bare soil it takes about 10 lbs. of seed for the same area. To scatter seeds more evenly, start broadcasting half of the amount in a North and South direction, and the other half in an East and West direction. Be sure and set your lawn mower higher for the first two months, so the grass will not be pulled-up before it is established. If you are in a new home, or have no lawn at all, it is best to plant rye now and wait until Spring to set out permanent lawn grass.

There is no economy in leaving old established lawns hungry during the colder months, for it will require fertilizer to get it back in shape next Spring. Feed at least half the usual amount you use during growing season, or give it about two or three good feedings of soluble plant food, using one of the attachments that fits on your garden hose.

* * *

You have to be on the lookout for the fall armyworm and the sod worms that damage your lawn considerably if not destroyed. Spray with DDT or Toxaphene.

* * *

Toxaphene or 40% Chlordane will also help the control of caterpillars or grasshoppers on Amaryllis and other plants. Use three tablespoonfuls to each gallon of water.

If you plant Amaryllis at this time, be sure and plant so the top of the bulb will be even with the ground. Some other bulbs that can be planted now include the following; Freesia, Calla (giant whites), Narcissus — for inside or shaded garden spots. Plant Narcissus, both types, from now thru December. Blooming time from 50 to 60 days. Keep planting Gladiolus every two weeks for extended bloom. Plant Ranunculus in pots, beds or borders in shaded spots. Plant one inch deep and three to four inches apart. Plant Anemones same way. Plant Darwin type Tulips in Tampa Bay area, from four to six inches deep and four to 12 inches apart. Some Iris can be planted now. Louisiana Iris are excellent for most areas of Florida except extreme Key section. The King Alfred yellow and the Mrs. E. H. Krelage white Daffodils can be planted now. Use them in beds or borders. See bulb charts for other bulbs that can be planted at this time.

The latter part of October usually starts off the rose season in North and Central Florida, and many nurseries offer started roses in large containers at this time. Most of the roses offered in packages are the older standards, and seldom do you find the newer ones available except through nurseries or from catalogs of Rose Specialists. Don't forget the old-fashioned Tea Roses that last for years with less trouble and less disease, etc. Thomasville Nurseries, of Thomasville, Ga. have some excellent ones for Florida and Gulf States.

* * *

Root-knot destroys many plants, and it generally makes its appearance in soil with very little or no humus. Some plants are immune, but many others are susceptible. If you discover weak looking, sickly plants with small flowers, deformed flowers or fruit, then pull-up a plant or dig deep enough to examine roots. If they are full of knotty warts then you had better get rid of them or treat with NEMAGON. Note: Some plants, shrubs and trees have roots with nitrogenous nodules that some people may mistake as root-knot, but you will not find these looking sickly or deformed, so it soon becomes easy to tell the difference. Cover crops, legumes, peanuts and others have nitrogenous roots. The Mothers Tongue (Albizzia lebbek) and the related Mimosa and others that are considered leguminous trees are helpful, and their roots must not be mistaken as root-knot.

* * *

The following herbs can be planted this month: Anise, Asparagus, Balm, Basil, Borage, Caraway, Cardoon, Celeriac, Chervil, Chicory, Chives, Coriander, Cress, Dill, Horehound, Leek, Marjoram, Parsley, Rhubarb, Roquette, Rue, Sage, Summer Savory, Thyme.

OCTOBER FLOWERS

Acrolinium (Small Strawflower)	Hunnemania
Ageratum	Lantana
Alyssum	Linaria
Asters	Lobelia
Arctotis	Lupin
Aubrietia (Rock Cress)	Marigold
Browallia (Amethyst)	Mignonette
Calendula	Myosotis
Calliopsis	Nasturtium
Campanula	Nemesia
Candytuft	Nemophila (Baby Blue Eyes)
Carnations	Nicotiana
Celosia (Cockscomb)	Nigella (Love in a Mist)
Centaurea (Cornflower)	Pansy
Clarkia	Petunia
Correopsis	Phlox
Cosmos	Poppy
Cynoglossum	Pyrethrum (Painted Daisy)
Delphinium (Larkspr ann.)	Salpiglossis
Dianthus (Pinks)	Salvia
Didiscus (Blue Lace Flower)	Scabiosa
Eschscholtzia (Calif. Poppy)	Schizanthus
Gaillardia	Shasta Daisy
Gerbera	Shirley Poppy
Gilia	Snapdragon
Godetia	Statice
Gypsophila	Stocks
Helichrysum (Strawflower)	Swan River Daisy
Hollyhock	Sweet Peas
	Sweet William
	Sweet Sultan
	Verbena
	Queen Anne's Lace

VEGETABLES

Beans	Garlic	Peas, English
Beets	Kale	Potatoes
Broccoli	Kohl Rabi	Radish
Brussel Sprouts	Leek	Rhubarb
Cabbage	Lettuce	Romaine
Carrots	Mustard	Rutabaga
Cauliflower	Onion Seed	Spinach
Celery	Onion Sets	Swiss Chard
Collard	Parsley	Turnips
Endive	Parsnips	

GRASSES AND FIELD SEEDS

Lupines	Rape	Rye
Clover (Sweet Kenland Red)		
Grasses (Bermuda, Bahia)		

Florida Planting Guide — November

If you haven't divided your Daylilies by now, then get busy and do so during November and early December. Although they will thrive if divided any month of the year, they make larger and more prolific plants if divided and reset in the Fall months. Many herbaceous perennials such as Angelonia, Dianthus (Pinks), Gerberas, Violets can be divided now.

Exotic Amazon (Eucharist) Lilies are one of the finest and easiest bulbous plants to grow, however they must be grown in very shady places, such as under trees and shrubs, with some sunlight trickling through a part of the day. They bloom during the Winter months as a rule and as late as March some years. The blooms are white and have a flaring cup in the center (lined with green) and are very fragrant. Leaves are long and wide. Bloom spikes are 18 inches or more in length. Many people grow Amazon lilies in tubs or large containers, and it seems they do better when their roots are constricted. Many are used as pot plants.

* * *

Time to plant Gloxinia bulbs this month and December. Planted now they should bloom by March.

* * *

In recent years the Regal Lily has done well in some areas of Florida and as far south as Sarasota. You might try some for either pot plants or for the outdoors. Same goes for Tulips.

* * *

GLORIOSA LILIES which are often termed Climbing Lilies are one of the finest and easiest of plants to grow in almost all areas of the state. Garden supply houses have them or you may get them from some of the catalogs and specialists mentioned on other pages. Choose a full sun or semi-shady place to grow them, and as they like to climb it is good to plant them near trees, fences, or trellis, etc. They also start from seeds. Large seed pods full of reddish-orange seeds are found on many vines after blooming season has finished and vines have almost dried up. Seeds are planted later, but use the tubers now.

Bulbs to plant now include: Glads, Amaryllis, Anemones, Freesias, White Callas, Dutch Tuilps, Easter Lilies, Ranunculus, Iris, Louisiana Iris, Narcissus, Gloriosa Lilies, Gloxinias, Regal Lilies, Amazon lilies.

* * *

STRAWFLOWERS are called Everlastings or Immortelles, and they are useful as garden subjects or as decorative material when dried. The majority of Everlastings belong in the Composite family and include the Helichrysum the most commonly known Strawflower and also the largest flower of this type, and the Acrolinium with smaller flowers. The Swan River Daisy, Helipterum, Xeranthemum (zeer-ANTH-em-um) or Immortelles are others of same group. Most common of the Strawflowers may be obtained in general run of seed packets offered, however you may have to get the others from a specialist in rare seeds, etc. One of the most commercial of the Everlastings is called STATICE and it is grown commercially in Pinellas County and other places in Florida. It belongs to the Limonium (Sea-Lavender) classification of the Leadwort or Plumbago family.

Mangoes should have a pre-bloom feeding from November 20th to December 15th. Use about one pound of calcium nitrate per foot of tree spread on dormant trees of bearing size. This should produce a good crop on the shy-bearing varieties, unless Anthracnose (fungus) is very bad. The old reliable Bordeaux mixture is good for Anthracnose. Another good formula is Dithane D-14 two quarts; zinc sulphate, one pound; hydrated lime, one-half pound to 100 gallons of water. Use a wetting agent such as Ortho liquid Spreader or B-1956. In seven days follow with another spraying. A good time to apply Anthracnose control is when first bloom clusters have appeared.

* * *

Feed AVOCADOS between November 15th and December 5th. Use a Nitrate of Soda and Potash formula 14-0-14 and use from 80 to 250 pounds per acre. Small trees need from 80 to 150 pounds per acre. These applications are very important for bloom development and fruit set.

* * *

If you didn't feed CITRUS in October, then apply a good commercial 3-6-8 or 3-6-10 special at the rate of one pound per feet of tree spread.

* * *

This is really the beginning of the ROSE planting time for most areas of Florida. Some consider December and January even better. Any of the three months would be suitable under most conditions, providing you use good stock. See article on Roses.

Florida Planting Guide — December

Time to plant Oriental Magnolias in North and portions of Central Florida. *Magnolia Souglangeana* or Chinese Saucer Magnolias are more or less large shrubs as compared to the *Magnolia grandiflora* that often reaches to 100 ft. in height, but they produce magnificent large blossoms of rosy-pink to purple color and with creamy-white petals within. The blossoms appear before leaves which are large and bright green in color, especially on the older plants. Nurseries in Northern part of Florida and South Georgia offer many of the Oriental Magnolias. Might add that they make nice cut flowers (with stem and branches) for vases and arrangements. Oriental types grow from eight to 20 feet.

December is also a good time to plant Azaleas and Camellias. Some blooms may be found on potted or balled plants, so that you may see what color you are getting. See article on Azaleas and Camellias for other instructions.

* * *

It is too late to plant the Floridii type Easter Lilies, but you may plant what is known as the Croft Easter Lily. There is another lily that looks like an Easter Lily, known as the Formosanum or Phillipine Lily that blooms through the hot months of July, August and September. In my own tests I have grown them year after year in Pinellas County, or St. Petersburg, Fla. Plant the bulbs now. They form large seed pods filled with hundreds of thin seeds that are collected from August through September and planted right away in about two or three years they make blooming plants. They grow in full sun, or better in semi-shady places.

* * *

The Butterfly or Buddleia bush are common plants in Georgia and other Southern States, but seldom found in Florida. However, there is a type from Africa known as *Buddleia Madagascariensis* that is extremely hardy and rambling in most all areas of Florida. This type has woolly twigs with a downy white or yellow on the underside. Leaves are bright to medium green and silvery underneath. Very profuse bloomer with either spikes of white flowers or with yellow flowers. May be pruned into shape (needs frequent shearing) or may be left to grow in sprawly vine-like manner. Grows almost anywhere except low wet places. Easy to start from cuttings. Blooms at frequent intervals.

Usually by December the ROSELLE (called Florida Cranberry Bush) has produced fleshy calyces that are ready to be picked and made into sauce similar to Cranberry Sauce, or for jelly. There is much confusion about the identity of the Roselle and a Red-Leaf Hibiscus or Mallow (*Hibiscus eetveldeanus*) that has many similar characteristics. The red-leaf hibiscus has all red leaves and stems, whereas the Roselle (*Hibiscus sabdariffa*) has red stems and branches, but the foliage is greenish, but may have a trace of red. The blossom of the red-leaf hibiscus is nearly all red, whereas the Roselle is yellow. Roselle calyces (short pods) become very fleshy and are tart, whereas the red-leaf hibiscus pods are more or less woody. Roselle jelly and sauce rates very high at the State and County Fairs. Seeds of the true Roselle may be obtained from the Kilgore Seed Co., Plant City, Fla. or Crenshaw McMichael Seed Co., Tampa, Fla. They are planted in March or April. Fruits ripen in 175 days.

* * *

The West Indies Yam vine dies down about December each year, and if you want to eat the underground tubers now or later, dig them now or next month. If left in the ground they will sprout and grow again next year. When the tubers are peeled and cooked like Irish Potatoes (boiled and buttered) they are similar in taste, but instead of a lot of starch, you have gluten. It is claimed that they are excellent for diabetics or for those who want to avoid too much starch. The tubers are rather rough-looking, but once they are peeled they are as nice in appearance as any Irish Potato. Some of the tubers reach up to 50 pounds. There are smaller tubers produced along the vine during the year, but are not edible and are used for seed. You can save them for long periods. West Indies Yams are true yams in the botanical sense, but no relation to the Sweet Potato which is often called yam. True botanical name is *Dioscorea alata*. There are many other Dioscoreas that are useful, but there is one that has similar vine appearance (but smooth tubers on vine) that is a pest. It is *Dioscorea bulbifera*. This one produces no underground tubers.

* * *

IPOMOEA SIDAEFOLIA VINE — Heavy rampart vine that produces many medium-sized white flowers (with green throat) resembling small moon flowers. Very spectacular in December.

NOVEMBER AND DECEMBER FLOWERS

Ageratum
Alyssum
Antirrhinum
    (Snapdragon)
Arctotis (Afr. Daisy)
Aster
Aubrietia (Rock Cress)
Balsam
Browallia (Amethyst)
Calendula
Calliopsis
Campanula
Candytuft
Carnation
Celosia (Cockscomb)
Centaurea
    (Cornflower)
Clarkia
Correopsis
Cosmos
Cynoglossum
Delphinium (Per.
    Larkspur)
Dianthus (Pinks)
Didiscus (Blue Lace
    Flower)
Echscholtzia
    (Calif. Poppy)
Gaillardia
Gerbera
Gilia
Godetia
Gypsophila
    ((Baby's Breath)

Helichrysum
    (Strawflower)
Hollyhock
Hunnemannia
Lantana
Larkspur
Linaria (Baby
    Snapdragon)
Lobelia
Lupin
Marigold
Mignonette
Myosotis
Nasturtium
Nemesia
Nemophila
Nigella
Pansy
Petunia
Phlox
Poppy
Pyrethrum
    (Painted Daisy)
Queen Anne's Lace
Schizanthus
Salvia
Scabiosa
Shasta Daisy
Snapdragon
Statice
Stocks
Sweet Peas
Sweet William
Verbena
Vinca (Periwinkle)

VEGETABLES

Beets
Broccoli
Brussel Sprouts
Cabbage
Carrots
Cauliflower
Celery
Collard
Eggplant
Endive
Garlic
Kale
Kohl Rabi
Leek
Lettuce

Mustard
Onion Seed
Onion Sets
Parsley
Peas, English
Pepper
Potatoes
Radish
Rhubarb (November)
Romaine
Rutabaga
Spinach
Swiss Chard
Turnip
Tomato (December)

GRASSES AND FIELD SEEDS

Clover, Crimson, Sweet
White, Ladino, Kenland
Red, Lupines, Oats.

Grasses, Italian Rye,
Carpet, Bahia, Rape,
Rye.

POINSETTIA — The glory of December and the Holiday Season. Red is most popular, white or pink Poinsettias are also available.

DOUBLE (also called triple) POINSETTIAS These grow in red shades.

Large flowers of the BOMBAX Tree (Bombax Malabaricum). One tree near Clearwater reaches to 125 feet. Miami area has a number of trees of this family including Chorisia. Pachira and Kapok. Blossoms are deep orange to red in color. Blooms from late December through January.